Hiking Grand Teton National Park

Second Edition

Bill Schneider

GUILFORD, CONNECTICUT
HELENA, MONTANA

AN IMPRINT OF THE GLOBE PEQUOT PRESS

FALCONGUIDES®

Copyright © 2005 Morris Book Publishing, LLC
A previous edition of this book was published in 1998 by
Falcon Publishing, Inc.

All photographs by the Bill Schneider unless otherwise
noted
Text design by Nancy Freeborn
Maps and elevation profiles by XNR Productions Inc.
© Morris Book Publishing, LLC

Library of Congress Cataloging-in-Publication Data
Schneider, Bill.
    Hiking Grand Teton National Park / Bill Schneider. —
2nd ed.
        p. cm. — (A Falcon Guide)
    ISBN 978-0-7627-2567-0
    1. Hiking — Wyoming — Grand Teton National Park —
Guidebooks. 2. Grand Teton National Park (Wyo.) — Guidebooks. I. Title. II. Series.
        GV199.42.W82G7367 2005
917.87'55 — dc22   2005040316

Manufactured in the United States of America
Second Edition/Third Printing

WILDERNESS is . . .

The FREEDOM to experience true wildness . . . to hear only nature's music . . . to study the little secrets of the natural world . . . and to enjoy the quiet and solitude so rare in the stressful life we now live.

The CHALLENGE to learn and respect wild country . . . to be self-reliant . . . to take your time . . . to test your physical abilities . . . to courteously share the last blank spots on the map with others . . . and to fully enjoy your wilderness experience while leaving no trace of your passing.

The OPPORTUNITY to discover why wilderness is priceless . . . to see the threats to your wilderness . . . to decide to devote part of yourself to preserving it . . . and to encourage others to do the same.

—Bill Schneider

Contents

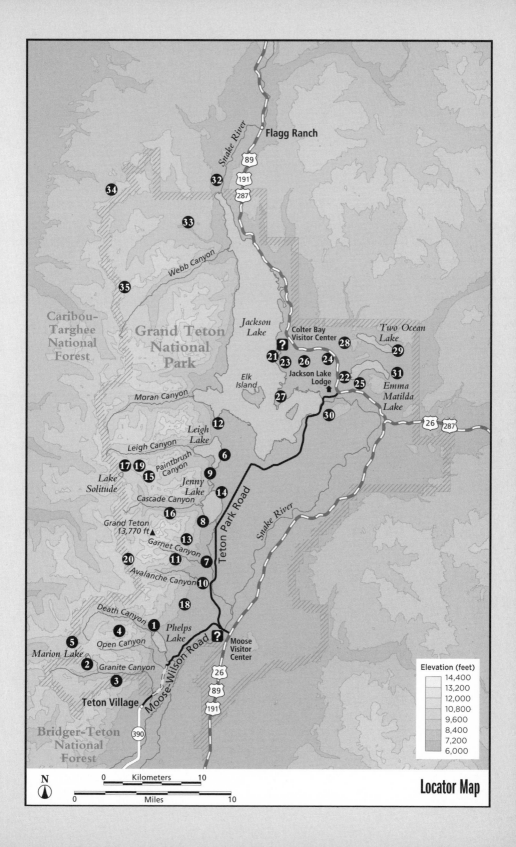

Flagg Ranch

Snake River

89
191
287

34

32

33

Webb Canyon

35

Caribou-
Targhee
National
Forest

Grand Teton
National
Park

Jackson
Lake

Colter Bay
Visitor Center

Two Ocean
Lake

?

21 23 26 24

28

29

Elk
Island

Jackson Lake
Lodge

22

25

31

Emma
Matilda
Lake

27

Moran Canyon

30

26 287

12

Leigh
Lake

Leigh Canyon

6

17 19

Paintbrush
Canyon

9

15

Jenny
Lake

14

Lake
Solitude

Cascade Canyon

16

8

Grand Teton
13,770 ft ▲

13

Garnet Canyon

7

20

11

Snake River

Avalanche Canyon

10

18

Death Canyon

1

Phelps
Lake

4

Open Canyon

5

2

Granite Canyon

Marion Lake

3

?

Moose
Visitor
Center

Moose-Wilson Road

Teton Park Road

26
89
191

Teton Village

390

Bridger-Teton
National
Forest

Elevation (feet)

14,400
13,200
12,000
10,800
9,600
8,400
7,200
6,000

N

0   Kilometers   10

0   Miles   10

Locator Map

North Trails Area

Acknowledgments

Most guidebooks, including this one, result from a combination of effort, not the work of one person.

I would like to thank the National Park Service for frequent cooperation in researching and reviewing this book, especially Katy Duffy, Don Burgette, Mark Mangleson, and Sara Petsch. Also, Sharlene Milligan and Jan Lynch from the Grand Teton Natural History Association were most helpful with their review and guidance.

I extend my gratitude to this book's first-edition editor, David Lee, for putting up with a difficult author, and my thanks go to production editor Jessica Solberg for overseeing the production of the first book. Also, thanks to Dave Paton for helping with the elevation profiles, Neil Sexton for the layout, and Eric West for the maps and elevation profiles. Thanks to Gillian Belnap, my editor for the second edition.

And, of course, what would I do without Marnie, Greg, and Heidi, my Schneider family hiking companions who kept me company on many long days and big hills while hiking the trails of Grand Teton? Thanks all.

Happy hikers on Hurricane Pass with Grand Teton and Middle Teton as a dramatic backdrop.

Introduction:
Hiking America's Most Famous Wilderness Skyline

Grand Teton National Park probably has the most famous wilderness skyline in the country. It shows up every year on millions of postcards, calendars, magazine and book covers, and television ads. But just looking at it is not enough. You need to go there and hike through the deep canyons gouged out by glaciers and over the big divides to feel the true essence of these mountains. For outstanding mountain scenery, Grand Teton ranks, quite simply, as the best. When you go there, you have to really try hard not to have a memorable hike. As you plan your trip, here are a few things you might want to know about hiking in Grand Teton National Park.

Prime season: The best time to hike Grand Teton is August and September. Snow buries the high peaks each winter, and it takes until mid-July to melt off, and sometimes until even later on high trails such as Hurricane Pass, Paintbrush Divide, and Moose Basin Divide.

Weather: It can snow any day of the year in Grand Teton, so always be prepared for it. The normal summer weather pattern (if there is such a thing) is clear mornings with thundershowers in the mid-afternoon, followed by clear, coolish evenings. This means early-morning hikers usually enjoy better weather, and they more often get their tents set up before it rains. June can frequently (but not always) be a fairly wet month in Grand Teton.

Sharing: Hikers don't have the trails of Grand Teton to themselves. They share those trails not only with a growing number of hikers and climbers but also with backcountry horse riders. If you meet a stock party on the trail, yield by moving off the trail on the downhill side and quietly let the stock animals pass.

Moose country: This is definitely moose country. In fact, it's difficult to go hiking all day in Grand Teton without seeing moose. Enjoying watching them, but stay out of the way. Moose do not yield to hikers.

Bears: Grand Teton has bears, both the common black bear and its larger, more cantankerous cousin, the grizzly. You probably won't see a grizzly, but as the bear population in the greater Yellowstone area grows, the number of grizzlies in Grand Teton will gradually increase. Grizzlies are, already, more common in the northern and less frequently used sections of the park, but all of Grand Teton should be considered grizzly country. And all bears—black and grizzly—are dangerous, so take all the standard precautions.

The canyons: Many hikes, such as Holly Lake (Hike 15), Cascade Canyon (Hike 16), and many others, leave the valley floor and penetrate the Teton Range via deep, glacier-scoured canyons. The canyons serve as pathways into the high peaks. They are usually steep in the first few miles, and then they level out and you're surrounded by steep-walled majesty on your way up a spectacular pass or divide.

Finding solitude: Grand Teton is so heavily used by hikers and climbers that in some places they seem to be everywhere. You can find solitude, however, especially in the North Trails area, as well as in a few other areas. (You probably will not find solitude at Lake Solitude.) If you want to be lonely for a change, check through the hike descriptions until you find a lightly used route.

Bugs: Perhaps the two seasons I hiked Grand Teton were off-years for the mosquito populations, but I have to say that there are fewer mosquitoes in Grand Teton than in most places in the Rocky Mountains. In the Beartooths or Yellowstone, the mosquitoes can block out the sun on a clear day, but in Grand Teton, I took out the repellent only once (in Glade Creek), which is unusual to say the least.

Large furry things on the road: When hurrying to get to the trailhead in the early morning hours or when feeling anxious while driving home in the evening, be especially watchful for large wildlife on the roadways. Hitting a moose or antelope will certainly ruin your day, and it's even harder on the animal.

Hiker friendly: In some national parks it's easy to feel overregulated. However, Grand Teton National Park has made special efforts to provide the freedom of choice and to limit the number of regulations.

Research pays: Plan your trip (and alternatives to it) before you get to Grand Teton. This saves valuable time—and you want to spend that time hiking instead of driving around or waiting in traffic jams, right? You may not be able to get the permit you had planned on, and bear management, forest fires, high water, road construction, and other factors can change things. You need a backup plan.

You can find details on many of these topics in the following pages.

Planning Your Trip

It's amazing how pleasant and stress-free your hiking trip to Grand Teton National Park can be when it's well planned. The following information should help you plan your trip.

Getting to Grand Teton National Park

Grand Teton National Park is in northwestern Wyoming, just south of Yellowstone National Park. You can drive to the park from Salt Lake City on Interstate 15 north to Logan, Utah, turning on U.S. Highway 89 through Idaho and Wyoming to Jackson, Wyoming, and Grand Teton National Park. You can also take U.S. Highway 26 east from Idaho Falls, Idaho, to Jackson or west from Dubois or Casper, Wyoming. From Montana, you can drive through Yellowstone National Park (slow but scenic) or take U.S. Highway 20 south of West Yellowstone, Montana, and turn off on Idaho Highways 32 and 33 over Teton Pass to Jackson, Wyoming.

Since federal highways pass through the park, you can see parts of Grand Teton without paying an entrance fee. Entrance stations are located on Teton Park Road just west of the Moose Visitor Center, at Moran Junction, and on Moose-Wilson

Road just south of the Granite Canyon Trailhead. Expect to pay a fee to enter the park at these stations.

The roads to the park are well maintained but only two lanes wide and often crowded with traffic, including slow-moving vehicles. If you drive during midday, don't be in a hurry. Unlike roads in neighboring Yellowstone National Park, the roads in Grand Teton are generally in good shape.

You can also fly to a small airport with limited jet service just north of Jackson, Wyoming. The airport is actually within the boundaries of the park.

Getting Backcountry Permits

In Grand Teton National Park, you must have a permit for all overnight use of the backcountry. Get these permits at visitor centers at Moose and Colter Bay and at the Jenny Lake Ranger Station. Be sure to ask the National Park Service for a back-country camping brochure that includes most of the basic information you need to get a permit. Call or write for a copy:

Backcountry Office
Grand Teton National Park
P.O. Drawer 170
Moose, WY 83012-0170
(307) 739–3309
(307) 739–3438 (fax)

Grand Teton has a backcountry permit reservation system, but only for one-third of the total sites. Designated sites can be reserved from January 1 through May 15 for $15 per trip, regardless of the number of people or the length of the trip. The National Park Service allows up to one-third of the designated sites to be reserved. Permits requested at park visitor centers and ranger stations are free but must be obtained no more than twenty-four hours before the start of your trip.

Reservations must be sent in by mail or fax to the backcountry office and can be applied for in person at the Moose Visitor Center, open daily from 8:00 A.M. to 5:00 P.M. Include the following information: name, address, daytime phone, number of people in your party, preferred campsites, and preferred dates. If possible, include alternate campsites and dates. The park service will send out a written confirmation. Phone reservations are not accepted, but you can get information by calling (307) 739–3309 or (307) 739–3397. Include a check with the permit request.

Your reservation holds your permit, but you still need to pick it up no later than 10:00 A.M. the day your trip starts. If you fail to pick it up by 10:00 A.M., it will become available to others. If you're running a little late, you can call ahead and the park service will hold your permit.

If you have a reservation but are unable to take the trip, be sure to notify the park service and cancel your reservation so the campsites can be made available to others. The park service does not issue refunds for cancellations.

Backcountry Camping Policy

Some national parks have policies that can hardly be described as "hiker friendly," and consequently it's easy to feel overregulated. However, Grand Teton has a hiker-friendly backcountry policy. For example, consider these long-range goals in the park's backcountry management plan:

- Provide visitors to the backcountry with a high-quality experience.
- Provide for a range of levels of solitude.
- Provide for visitor use of the backcountry with a minimum level of restrictions.
- Provide hikers in pristine areas with the opportunity to have the same type of wilderness experience that people would have had before Europeans arrived in this area.

To allow more people to enjoy the backcountry, the park service limits use for each hiker to no more than two nights in the same campsite and to ten nights per summer. Quotas are set to prevent overuse, and party size is limited to six people. If you have a larger party (up to twelve allowed), you must camp at a designated group site.

In 1973 the park service banned all campfires in the park above 7,000 feet elevation. Only designated, low-elevation sites have fire grills where campfires can be built.

Backcountry camping is allowed in camping zones and at designated sites at backcountry lakes like Lake Marion and Holly Lake. Within each camping zone are "indicated" campsites. The sites are usually convenient and well placed. While visiting a camping zone, you are not required to stay in an indicated campsite. You can set up a no-impact camp anywhere in a camping zone. In some cases, the park service also allows off-trail camping outside of camping zones.

Backcountry Use Regulations

Backcountry use regulations aren't intended to complicate your life. They help preserve the natural landscape and protect park visitors. The following backcountry use regulations are distributed to hikers when they get their permits.

In Grand Teton, you must do the following:

- Have a permit for all overnight stays in the backcountry.
- Carefully follow the instructions on the permit.
- Build campfires only in designated fire pits at certain low-elevation campsites.
- Use only collected dead and downed wood. Keep fires small, and do not leave them unattended. Backpacking stoves are encouraged.
- Use food storage poles or boxes or suspend food at least 10 feet above the ground and 4 feet horizontally from a post or tree.
- Carry out all trash. If you can pack it in, you can pack it out.
- Have a valid Wyoming state fishing permit if you're fishing the waters of Grand Teton.

Enjoying the last moments of the day on the shore of Phelps Lake.

In Grand Teton, you must not do any of the following:
- Feed, touch, tease, frighten, or intentionally disturb wildlife.
- Take pets into the backcountry.
- Make campsite "improvements" such as fire rings, rock walls, log benches, drainage, trenches, etc.
- Possess or operate a motorized vehicle, bicycle, wheeled vehicle, or cart in any undeveloped area or on any backcountry trail.
- Dispose of human waste within 200 feet of any water source or campsite or within sight of a trail.
- Possess, destroy, injure, deface, remove, dig, or disturb from its natural state any plant, rock, animal, mineral, cultural, or archaeological resource.
- Use or possess weapons, traps, or nets.
- Cut switchbacks.
- Wash dishes or bathe in park streams or lakes.

Climbing up to the Static Peak Divide.

For More Information

For a great summary of basic facts on visiting Grand Teton, call the main park number and ask for a copy of *Teewinot,* a free newspaper published by the Grand Teton Natural History Association. You can also get a copy at the entrance station when you enter the park. The paper contains a list of commercial services available in and near the park, updates on park road construction, lists of ranger-led activities, events and guided tours, campgrounds, medical and emergency services and facilities, area museums, special exhibits, plus lots more useful information. *Teewinot* will answer most of your questions about park services. Because of budget cuts, the park service is sometimes unable to keep up with all visitor inquiries, so please be patient when trying to get your questions answered. There are many books and other publications about Grand Teton that provide a wealth of excellent information, and they often provide a better way to get information than calling the park service directly. Many of these publications are available at park visitor centers.

Contact the park service at this address and phone number:

National Park Service
Park Headquarters
P.O. Drawer 170
Moose, WY 83012-0170
(307) 739–3309
www.nps.gov/grte

Emergency Medical Services

In case of an emergency, call 911. You can also call the park's main dispatch number (307–739–3300) to report an emergency. Because of its remote location, the park has limited medical facilities. You also can find limited care facilities at the Grand Teton Medical Clinic at Jackson Lake Lodge and at St. John's Hospital in Jackson, Wyoming.

Using This FalconGuide

To help you choose a hike, we preface each entry with some basic information, including type of hike, difficulty ratings, and distance covered. Our basic maps and elevation profiles supplement this information with quick visuals. To use these tools effectively, please note the explanations below.

Types of Hikes

Hikes in this FalconGuide have been organized into the following categories:

Loop: Starts and finishes at the same trailhead, with no (or very little) retracing of your steps. Sometimes the definition of loop is stretched to include "lollipops" and trips that involve a short walk on a road at the end of the hike to get back to your vehicle.

Shuttle: A point-to-point trip that requires two vehicles (one left at each end of the trail) or a prearranged pickup at a designated time and place. One good way to manage the logistical problems of shuttles is to arrange for another party to start at the other end of the trail. The two parties meet at a predetermined point and then trade keys. When finished, they drive each other's vehicles home.

Out and back: Traveling to a specific destination, then retracing your steps back to the trailhead.

Base camp: Any hike on which you spend several nights at the same campsite, using the extra days for fishing, relaxing, or day hiking.

Hike Ratings

To help you plan your trip, trails are rated by difficulty. However, difficulty ratings for trails serve only as general guides, not the final word. What is difficult to one hiker may be easy to another. In this guidebook, difficulty ratings take into account both how long and how strenuous a route is. Following are general definitions of the ratings.

Long footbridge over marshy Third Creek on the Willow Flats Loop hike.

Easy: Suitable for any hiker, including children or elderly people, without serious elevation gain, hazardous sections, or places where the trail is faint.

Moderate: Suitable for hikers who have some experience and at least an average fitness level. Probably not suitable for children or the elderly unless they have an above-average level of fitness. The hike may have some short sections where the trail is difficult to follow, and it often includes some hills.

Difficult: Suitable for experienced hikers with above-average fitness level, often with sections of the trail that are difficult to follow or even some off-trail sections that could require knowledge of route-finding with a topo map and compass, sometimes with serious elevation gain and possibly some hazardous conditions.

Campsite Ratings

In several instances, I refer to campsites as "five-star," "four-star," "three-star," etc. This generally describes my nonscientific evaluation of the campsite but does not relate to any statistical standard. Five-star campgrounds, like top hotels and restaurants, rank among the best available.

Distances

In this guidebook most distances come from park service signs and brochures, but some trail mileage is estimated. Since it's so difficult and time consuming to precisely measure trails, most distances listed in any guidebook, on trail signs, and in park brochures are usually estimates. In Grand Teton you may find minor inconsistencies between signs, brochures, and this book, but these are rarely significant.

Keep in mind that distance is often less important than difficulty. A rocky, 2-mile, uphill trail can take longer and require more effort than 4 miles on a well-contoured trail on flat terrain. The moral is this: Don't get too excited if the distance is slightly off.

Maps

The maps in this book use elevation tints, called hypsometry, to portray relief. Each gray tone represents a range of equal elevation gain and loss. The darker tones are lower elevations and the lighter grays are higher elevations. The lighter the tone, the higher the elevation. Narrow bands of different gray tones spaced closely together indicate steep terrain, whereas wider bands indicate areas of more gradual slope.

These maps serve as general guides only. They do not have enough detail and do not cover enough territory to be used on their own in the field. You definetly should take a better map with you on any hike.

Elevation Profiles

This book uses elevation profiles to provide an idea of the length and elevation of hills you will encounter along each hike. In each of the profiles, the vertical axes of the graphs show the distance climbed in feet. In contrast, the horizontal axes show the distance traveled in miles. It is important to understand that the vertical (feet) and horizontal (miles) scales can differ between hikes. Read each profile carefully, making sure you read both the height and distance shown. This will help you interpret what you see in each profile. Some elevation profiles may show gradual hills to be steep or steep hills to be gradual. Elevation profiles are not provided for hikes with little or no elevation gain.

Zero Impact

Going into a national park such as Grand Teton is like visiting a famous museum. You obviously do not want to leave your mark on an art treasure in the museum. If everybody going through the museum leaves one little mark, the piece of art will be quickly destroyed—and of what value is a big building full of trashed art? The same goes for a pristine wilderness such as Grand Teton, which is as magnificent as any masterpiece by any artist. If we all leave just one little mark on the landscape, the wilderness will soon be despoiled.

A wilderness can accommodate human use as long as everybody behaves, but a few thoughtless or uninformed visitors can ruin it for everybody who follows. All wilderness users have a responsibility to know and follow the rules of no-trace camping. An important source of these guidelines, including the most updated research, can be found in the book *Leave No Trace*.

Today most wilderness users want to walk softly, but some aren't aware that they have poor manners. Often their actions are dictated by the outdated habits of a previous generation of campers who cut green boughs for evening shelters, built campfires with fire rings, and dug trenches around tents. In the 1950s these "camping rules" may have been acceptable, but they leave long-lasting scars and today such behavior is absolutely unacceptable. The wilderness is shrinking, and the number of users is mushrooming. More and more camping areas show unsightly signs of heavy use.

Consequently, a new code of ethics is growing out of the necessity of coping with the unending waves of people who want a perfect wilderness experience. Today we all must leave no clues that we have gone before. Canoeists can look behind the canoe and see no trace of their passing. Hikers, mountain bikers, and four-wheelers should have the same goal. Enjoy the wilderness, but leave no trace of your visit.

Three FalconGuide Principles of Zero Impact

- Leave with everything you brought.
- Leave no sign of your visit.
- Leave the landscape as you found it.

Most of us know better than to litter—in or out of the wilderness. Be sure you leave nothing, regardless of how small it is, along the trail or at the campsite. This means you should pack out everything, including orange peels, flip tops, cigarette butts, and gum wrappers. Also, pick up any trash that others leave behind.

Follow the main trail. Avoid cutting switchbacks and walking on vegetation beside the trail.

Don't pick up "souvenirs," such as rocks, antlers, or wildflowers. The next person wants to see them, too, and collecting such souvenirs violates park regulations.

Avoid making loud noises that may disturb others. Remember, sound travels easily to the other side of the lake. Be courteous.

Carry a lightweight trowel to bury human waste 6 to 8 inches deep, and pack out used toilet paper. Keep human waste at least 200 feet from any water source.

Finally, and perhaps most importantly, strictly follow the pack-in/pack-out rule. If you carry something into the backcountry, consume it or carry it out.

Zero impact—and put your ear to the ground in the wilderness and listen carefully. Thousands of people coming behind you are thanking you for your courtesy and good sense.

Make It a Safe Trip

The Boy Scouts of America have been guided for decades by what is perhaps the best single piece of safety advice: "Be Prepared!" For starters, this means carrying survival and first-aid materials, proper clothing, compass, and topographic map—and knowing how to use them.

Perhaps the second-best piece of safety advice is to tell somebody where you're going and when you plan to return. Pilots must file flight plans before every trip, and anybody venturing into a blank spot on the map should do the same. File your "flight plan" with a friend or relative before taking off.

Close behind your flight plan and being prepared with proper equipment is physical conditioning. Being fit not only makes wilderness travel more fun, but it also makes it safer. To whet your appetite for more knowledge of wilderness safety and preparedness, following are a few more tips:

- Check the weather forecast. Be careful not to get caught at high altitude by a bad storm or along a stream in a flash flood. Watch cloud formations closely so you don't get stranded on a ridgeline during a lightning storm. Avoid traveling during prolonged periods of cold weather.
- Avoid traveling alone in the wilderness.
- Keep your party together.
- Study basic survival and first aid before leaving home.
- Don't eat wild plants unless you have positively identified them.
- Before you leave for the trailhead, find out as much as you can about the route, especially the potential hazards.
- Don't exhaust yourself or other members of your party by traveling too far or too fast. Let the slowest person set the pace.
- Don't wait until you're confused to look at your maps. Follow them as you go along, from the moment you start moving up the trail, so you have a continual fix on your location.
- If you get lost, don't panic. Sit down and relax for a few minutes while you carefully check your topo map and take a reading with your compass. Confidently plan your next move. It's often smart to retrace your steps until you find familiar ground, even if you think it might lengthen your trip. Lots of people get temporarily lost in the wilderness and survive—usually by calmly and rationally dealing with the situation.
- Stay clear of all wild animals.
- Take a first-aid kit that includes, at a minimum, the following items: sewing needle, snakebite kit, aspirin, antibacterial ointment, two antiseptic swabs, two butterfly bandages, adhesive tape, four adhesive strips, four gauze pads, two triangular bandages, codeine tablets, two inflatable splints, Moleskin or Second Skin for blisters, one roll of 3-inch gauze, a CPR shield, rubber gloves, and lightweight first-aid instructions.
- Take a survival kit that includes, at a minimum, the following items: compass, whistle, matches in a waterproof container, cigarette lighter, candle, signal mir-

ror, flashlight, fire starter, aluminum foil, water purification tablets, space blanket, and flare.

- Last but not least, don't forget that the best defense against unexpected hazards is knowledge. Read up on the latest in wilderness safety information. The Globe Pequot Press offers a extensive list, including *Wilderness First Responder, Wilderness Survival,* and *Wilderness Predators of the Rockies.* (Call 800–243–0495 for a free catalog.)

Lightning: You Might Never Know What Hit You

The high-altitude topography of Grand Teton is prone to sudden thunderstorms, especially in July and August. If you get caught by a lightning storm, take special precautions. Remember the following:

- Lightning can travel far ahead of a storm, so be sure to take cover before the storm hits.
- Don't try to make it back to your vehicle. It isn't worth the risk. Instead, seek shelter even if it's only a short way back to the trailhead. Lightning storms usually don't last long, and from a safe vantage point, you might enjoy the sights and sounds.
- Be especially careful not to get caught on a mountaintop or exposed ridge; under large, solitary trees; in the open; or near standing water.
- Seek shelter in a low-lying area, ideally in a dense stand of small, uniformly sized trees.
- Stay away from anything that might attract lightning, such as metal tent poles, graphite fishing rods, or pack frames.
- Get in a crouch position and place both feet firmly on the ground.
- Don't walk or huddle together. Instead, stay 50 feet apart, so if somebody gets hit by lightning, others in your party can give first aid.
- If you're in a tent, stay there, in your sleeping bag on your sleeping pad.

Hypothermia: The Silent Killer

Be aware of the danger of hypothermia—a condition in which the body's internal temperature drops below normal. It can lead to mental and physical collapse and death.

Hypothermia is caused by exposure to cold and is aggravated by wetness, wind, and exhaustion. The moment you begin to lose heat faster than your body produces it, you're suffering from exposure. Your body starts involuntary exercise, such as shivering, to stay warm and makes involuntary adjustments to preserve normal temperature in vital organs, restricting blood flow to the extremities. Both responses drain your energy reserves. The only way to stop the drain is to reduce the degree of exposure.

With full-blown hypothermia, as energy reserves are exhausted cold reaches

Mount Moran across Heron Pond on the Hermitage Point Trail.

the brain, depriving you of good judgment and reasoning power. You won't be aware that this is happening. You lose control of your hands. Your internal temperature slides downward. Without treatment, this slide leads to stupor, collapse, and death.

To defend against hypothermia, stay dry. When clothes get wet, they lose about 90 percent of their insulating value. Wool loses relatively less heat; cotton, down, and some synthetics lose more. Choose rain clothes that cover the head, neck, body, and legs and provide good protection against wind-driven rain. Most hypothermia cases develop in air temperatures between 30 and 50 degrees F, but hypothermia can develop in warmer temperatures.

If your party is exposed to wind, cold, and wet, think hypothermia. Watch yourself and others for these symptoms: uncontrollable fits of shivering; vague, slow, slurred speech; memory lapses; incoherence; immobile, fumbling hands; frequent stumbling or a lurching gait; drowsiness (to sleep is to die); apparent exhaustion; and inability to get up after a rest. When a member of your party has hypothermia, he

Big meadows of Lower Berry Creek.

or she may deny any problem. Believe the symptoms, not the victim. Even mild symptoms demand treatment, as follows:

- Get the victim out of the wind and rain.
- Strip off all wet clothes.
- If the victim is only mildly impaired, give him or her warm drinks. Then get the victim in warm clothes and a warm sleeping bag. Place well-wrapped water bottles filled with heated water close to the victim.
- If the victim is badly impaired, attempt to keep him or her awake. Put the victim in a sleeping bag with another person—both naked. If you have a double bag, put two warm people in with the victim.

Be Bear Aware

The first step of any hike in bear country is an attitude adjustment. Nothing guarantees total safety. Hiking in bear country such as Grand Teton National Park adds a small additional risk to your trip. That risk can be greatly minimized, however, by adhering to this age-old piece of advice: Be prepared. And being prepared doesn't only mean having the right equipment. It also means having the right information. Knowledge is your best defense.

You can—and should—thoroughly enjoy your trip to bear country. Don't let the fear of bears ruin your experience. This fear can accompany you every step of the way. It can be constantly lurking in the back of your mind, preventing you from enjoying the wildest and most beautiful places left on Earth. And even worse, some bear experts think bears might actually be able to sense your fear.

Being prepared and being knowledgeable gives you confidence. It allows you to fight back the fear that can burden you throughout your stay in bear country. You won't—nor should you—forget about bears and the basic rules of safety, but proper preparation allows you to keep the fear of bears at bay and let enjoyment rule the day.

On top of that, do we really want to be totally safe? If we did, we probably would never go hiking in the wilderness—bears or no bears. We certainly wouldn't, at much greater risk, drive hundreds of miles to get to the trailhead. Perhaps a tinge of danger adds a desired element to our wilderness trip.

Hiking in Bear Country

Nobody likes surprises, and bears dislike them, too. The majority of bear maulings occur when a hiker surprises a bear. Therefore, it's vital to do everything possible to avoid these surprise meetings. Perhaps the best way is to know the five-part system. If you follow these five rules, the chance of encountering a bear on the trail sinks to the slimmest possible margin.

- Be alert.
- Go in with a group and stay together.
- Stay on the trail.
- Hike in the middle of the day.
- Make noise.

No substitute for alertness: As you hike, watch ahead and to the sides. Don't fall into the all-too-common and particularly nasty habit of fixating on the trail 10 feet ahead. It's especially easy to do this when dragging a heavy pack up a long hill or when carefully watching your step on a heavily eroded trail.

Using your knowledge of bear habitat and habits, be especially alert in areas most likely to be frequented by bears, such as avalanche chutes, berry patches, along streams, and through stands of whitebark pine.

Watch carefully for bear signs and be especially watchful (and noisy) if you see any. If you see a track or a scat, but it doesn't look fresh, pretend it's fresh. The area is obviously frequented by bears.

Watch the wind: The wind can be a friend or foe. The strength and direction of the wind can make a significant difference in your chances of an encounter with a bear. When the wind is blowing at your back, your smell travels ahead of you, alerting any bear that might be on or near the trail ahead. Conversely, when the wind

Footbridge over Third Creek on Willow Flats Loop hike.

blows in your face, your chances of a surprise meeting with a bear increase, so make more noise and be more alert.

A strong wind can also be noisy and limit a bear's ability to hear you coming. If a bear can't smell or hear you coming, the chances of an encounter greatly increase, so watch the wind.

Safety in numbers: There have been very few instances where a large group has had an encounter with a bear. On the other hand, a large percentage of hikers mauled by bears were hiking alone. Large groups naturally make more noise and put out more smell and probably appear more threatening to bears. In addition, if you're hiking alone and get injured, there is nobody to go for help. For these reasons, rangers in Grand Teton recommend parties of four or more hikers when going into bear country.

When a large party splits up, it becomes two small groups and the advantage is lost, so stay together. If you're on a family hike, keep the kids from running ahead. If you're in a large group, keep the stronger members from going ahead or weaker members from lagging behind. The best way to prevent this natural separation is to ask one the slowest members of the group to lead. This keeps everybody together.

Stay on the trail: Although bears use trails, they don't often use them during midday when hikers commonly use them. Through generations of associating trails with people, bears probably expect to find hikers on trails, especially during midday.

Contrarily, bears probably don't expect to find hikers off trails. Bears rarely settle down in a day bed right along a heavily used trail. If you wander around in thickets off the trail, however, you are more likely to stumble into an occupied day bed or cross paths with a traveling bear.

Sleeping late: Bears—and most other wildlife—usually aren't active during the middle of a day, especially on a hot summer day. Wild animals are most active around dawn and dusk. Therefore, hiking early in the morning or late afternoon increases your chances of seeing wildlife, including bears. Likewise, hiking during midday on a hot August day greatly reduces the chance of an encounter.

Sounds: Perhaps the best way to avoid a surprise meeting with a bear is to make sure the bear knows you're coming, so make lots of noise. Some experts think metallic noise is superior to human voices, which can be muffled by natural conditions, but the important issue is making lots of noise, regardless of what kind of noise.

Running: Many avid runners like to get off paved roads and running tracks and onto backcountry trails. But running on trails in bear country can be seriously hazardous to your health.

Leave the night to the bears: Like running on trails, hiking at night can be very risky. Bears are more active after dark, and you can't see them until it's too late. If you get caught at night, be sure to make lots of noise, and remember that bears commonly travel on hiking trails at night.

You can be dead meat, too: If you see or smell a carcass of a dead animal when hiking, immediately vacate the area. Don't let your curiosity keep you near the carcass a second longer than necessary. Bears commonly hang around a carcass, guarding it and feeding on it for days until it's completely consumed. Your presence could easily be interpreted as a threat to the bear's food supply, and a vicious attack could be imminent.

If you see a carcass ahead of you on the trail, don't go any closer. Instead, abandon your hike and return to the trailhead. If the carcass is between you and the trailhead, take a very long detour around it, upwind from the carcass, making lots of noise along the way. Be sure to report the carcass to the local ranger. This might prompt a temporary trail closure or special warnings and prevent injury to other hikers. Rangers will, in some cases, go in and drag the carcass away from the trail.

Cute, cuddly, and lethal: If you see a bear cub, don't go one inch closer to it. It might seem abandoned, but it most likely is not. Mother bear is probably very close, and female bears fiercely defend their young.

It doesn't do you any good in your pack: If you brought a repellent such as pepper spray, don't bury it in your pack. Keep it as accessible as possible. Most pepper spray comes in a holster or somehow conveniently attaches to your belt or pack.

Such protection won't do you any good if you can't have it ready to fire in one or two seconds. Before hitting the trail, read the directions carefully and test fire the spray.

Regulations: Nobody likes rules and regulations. National parks have a few that you must follow, however. These rules aren't meant to take the freedom out of your trip. They are meant to help bring you back safely.

But I didn't see any bears: Now, you know how to be safe. Walk up the trail constantly clanging two metal pans together. It works every time. You won't see a bear, but you'll hate your "wilderness experience." You left the city to get away from loud noise.

Yes, you can be very safe, but how safe do you want to be and still be able to enjoy your trip? It's a balancing act. First, be knowledgeable and then decide how far you want to go. Everybody has to make his or her own personal choice.

Here's another conflict. If you do everything listed here, you most likely will not see any bears—or any deer or moose or eagles or any other wildlife. Again, you make the choice. If you want to be as safe as possible, follow these rules religiously. If you want to see wildlife, including bears, do all of this in reverse, but then, you are increasing your chances of an encounter instead of decreasing it.

Camping in Bear Country

Staying overnight in bear country is not dangerous, but it adds a slight additional risk to your trip. The main difference is the presence of more food, cooking and garbage. Plus, you are in bear country at night when bears are usually most active. Once again, however, following a few basic rules greatly minimizes this risk.

Storing food and garbage: If the campsite doesn't have a heavy, metal, bear-resistant storage box or bear pole, be sure to locate a good hanging tree before it gets dark. It's not only difficult to store food after darkness falls, but it's easier to forget some juicy morsel on the ground. Also, be sure to store food in airtight, waterproof bags to prevent food odors from circulating throughout the forest. For double protection, put food and garbage in zip-lock bags and then seal tightly in a larger plastic bag.

Most camping zones in Grand Teton have bear-resistant lockers for food storage, but in a few cases, you may have to hang food. For these situations, the backcountry rangers in Grand Teton recommend a counterbalance system. Backpackers receive instructions on this system when they get their backcountry camping permit.

Special equipment: It's not really that special, but one piece of equipment you definitely need is a good supply of zip-lock bags. This handy invention is perfect for keeping food smell to a minimum and helps keep food from spilling on your pack, clothing, or other gear.

Climbing down to Death Canyon from the Static Peak Divide. ▶

Take a special bag for storing food. The bag must be sturdy and waterproof. You can get dry bags at most outdoor specialty stores, but you can get by with a trash compactor bag. Regular garbage bags can break and leave your food spread on the ground.

You also need 100 feet of nylon cord. You don't need a heavy climbing rope to store food. Go light instead. Parachute cord will usually suffice unless you plan to hang large quantities of food and gear (which might be the case on a long back-packing excursion with a large group).

You can also buy a small pulley system to make hoisting a heavy load easier. Again, you can usually get by without this extra weight in your pack unless you have a massive load to hang.

What to hang: To be as safe as possible, store everything that has any food smell. This includes cooking gear, eating utensils, bags used to keep food in your pack, all garbage, and even clothes with food smells on them. If you spilled something on your clothes, change into other clothes for sleeping and hang clothes with food smells with the food and garbage. If you take them into the tent, you aren't separating your sleeping area from food smells. Try to keep food odors off your pack, but if you failed, put the food bag inside and hang the pack.

What to keep in your tent: You can't be too careful in keeping food smells out of the tent. Just in case a bear has become accustomed to coming into that campsite looking for food, it's vital to keep all food smells out of the tent. This often includes your pack, which is hard to keep odor-free. Usually only take valuables (like cameras and binoculars), clothing, and sleeping gear into the tent.

If you brought a bear repellent, such as pepper spray, sleep with it. Also, keep a flashlight in the tent. If an animal comes into camp and wakes you up, you need the flashlight to identify it.

The campfire: Regulations prohibit campfires in most campsites in Grand Teton, but if you're in an area where fires are allowed, treat yourself. Besides adding the nightly entertainment, the fire might make your camp safer from bears.

The campfire provides the best possible way to get rid of food smells. Build a small but hot fire and thoroughly burn everything that smells of food—garbage, left-overs, fish entrails, everything. If you brought food in cans or other incombustible containers, burn them, too. You can even dump extra water from cooking or dish water on the edge of the fire to erase the smell.

Be very sure you have the fire hot enough to completely burn everything. If you leave partially burned food scraps in the fire, you are setting up a dangerous situation for the next camper to use this site.

Before leaving camp the next morning, dig out the fire pit and pack out anything that has not completely burned, even if you believe it no longer carries food smells. For example, many foods like dried soup or hot chocolate come in foil packages that might seem like they burn, but they really don't. Pack out the scorched foil and cans (now with very minor food smells). Also, pack out foil and cans left by other campers.

Sunset Lake in the Alaska Basin.

Types of food: Don't get paranoid about the types of food you bring. All food has some smell, and you can make your trip much less enjoyable by fretting too much over food.

Perhaps the safest option is freeze-dried food. It carries very little smell, and it comes in convenient envelopes that allow you to "cook it" by merely adding boiling water. This means you don't have cooking pans to wash or store. However, freeze-dried food is very expensive, and many backpackers don't use it—and still safely enjoy bear country.

Dry, prepacked meals (often pasta- or rice-based) offer an affordable compromise to freeze-dried foods. Also, take your favorite high-energy snack and don't worry about it. Avoid fresh fruit and canned meats and fish.

The key point is this: What food you have along is much less critical than how you handle it, cook it, and store it. A can of tuna fish might put out a smell, but if you eat all of it in one meal, don't spill it on the ground or on your clothes, and burn the can later, it can be quite safe.

Hanging food at night is not the only storage issue. Also, make sure you place food correctly in your pack. Use airtight packages as much as possible. Store food in

The north section of the Teton Range with Third Creek in the foreground.

the containers it came in or, when opened, in zip-lock bags. This keeps food smells out of your pack and off your other camping gear and clothes.

How to cook: The overriding philosophy of cooking in bear country is to create as little odor as possible. Keep it simple. Use as few pans and dishes as possible. Unless it's a weather emergency, don't cook in the tent. If you like winter backpacking, you probably cook in the tent, but you should have a different tent for summer backpacking.

If you can have a campfire and decide to cook fish, try cooking in aluminum foil envelopes instead of frying them. Then, after removing the cooked fish, quickly and completely burn the fish scraps off the foil. Using foil also means you don't have to wash the pan you used to cook the fish.

Be careful not to spill on yourself while cooking. If you do, change clothes and hang the clothes with food odor with the food and garbage. Wash your hands thoroughly before retiring to the tent.

Don't cook too much food, so you don't have to deal with leftovers. If you do end up with extra food, however, you only have two choices. Carry it out or burn it. Don't bury it or throw it in a lake or leave it anywhere in bear country. A bear will most likely find and dig up any food or garbage buried in the backcountry.

Taking out the garbage: In bear country, you have only two choices—burn garbage or carry it out. Prepare for garbage problems before you leave home. Bring along airtight zip-lock bags to store garbage. Be sure to hang your garbage at night along with your food. Also, carry in as little garbage as possible by discarding excess packaging while packing.

Washing dishes: This is a sticky problem, but there is one easy solution. If you don't dirty dishes, you don't have to wash them. So try to minimize food smell by using as few dishes and pans as possible—and wash them as soon as you finish with them. If you use the principles of no-trace camping, you are probably doing as much as you can to reduce food smell from dishes.

If you brought paper towels, use one to carefully remove food scraps from pans and dishes before washing them. Then, when you wash dishes, you have much less food smell. Burn the dirty towels or store them in zip-lock bags with other garbage. Put pans and dishes in zip-lock bags before putting them back in your pack.

If you end up with lots of food scraps in the dish water, drain out the scraps and store them in zip-lock bags with other garbage or burn them. You can bring a light-weight screen to filter out food scraps from dish water, but be sure to store the screen with the food and garbage. If you have a campfire, pour the dish water around the edge of the fire. If you don't have a fire, take the dishwater at least 200 feet down-wind and downhill from camp and pour it on the ground or in a small hole. Don't put dish water or food scraps in a lake or stream.

Although possibly counter to accepted rules of cleanliness for many people, you can skip washing dishes altogether on the last night of your trip. Instead, simply use the paper towels to clean the dirty dishes as much as possible. You can wash them when you get home. Pack dirty dishes in zip-lock bags before putting them back in your pack.

Finally, don't put it off. Do dishes immediately after eating, so a minimum of food smell lingers in the area.

Choosing a tent site: Try to keep your tent site at least 100 feet from your cooking area. In Grand Teton, unfortunately, some campsites do not adequately separate the cooking area from the tent site. Store food at least 100 yards from the tent. You can store it near the cooking area to further concentrate food smells.

Not under the stars: Some people prefer to sleep out under the stars instead of using a tent. This might be okay in areas not frequented by bears, but it's not a good idea in bear country. The thin fabric of a tent certainly isn't any real physical pro-tection from a bear, but it does present a psychological barrier to a bear that wants to come even closer.

Do somebody a big favor: Report all bear sightings to the ranger after your trip. This might not help you, but it could save another camper's life. If rangers get enough reports to spot a pattern, they manage the area to prevent potentially haz-ardous situations.

Soaking in the view from a sandy beach along the east shore of Leigh Lake, with Mount St. John and Rockchuck Peak as a backdrop.

The Bear Essentials of Hiking and Camping

- Respect any warning signs posted by agencies.
- Knowledge is the best defense.
- There is no substitute for alertness.
- Hike with a large group and stay together.
- Don't hike alone in bear country.
- Stay on the trail.
- Hike in the middle of the day.
- Make lots of noise while hiking.
- Never approach a bear.
- Females with cubs are very dangerous.
- Stay away from carcasses.
- Defensive hiking works. Try it.

- Choose a safe campsite.
- Camp below timberline.
- Separate sleeping and cooking areas.
- Sleep in a tent.
- Cook just the right amount of food and eat it all.
- Store food and garbage out of reach of bears.
- Never feed bears.
- Keep food odors out of the tent.
- Leave no food rewards for bears.

Be Aware of Mountain Lions, Too

The most important safety element for recreation in mountain lion country is simply recognizing their habitat. Mountain lions primarily feed on deer, so these common ungulates are a key element in cougar habitat. Fish and wildlife agencies usually have good information about deer distribution from population surveys and hunting results.

Basically, where you have a high deer population, you can expect to find mountain lions.

Deer tracks can be found easily on dirt roads and trails. If you are not familiar with identifying deer tracks, seek the advice of someone knowledgeable, or refer to a book on animal tracks such as *Scats and Tracks of the Rocky Mountains* published by The Globe Pequot Press.

Safety Guidelines for Traveling in Mountain Lion Country

To stay as safe as possible when hiking in mountain lion country, follow this advice.

- Travel with a friend or group. There's safety in numbers, so stay together.
- Don't let small children wander away by themselves.
- Don't let pets run unleashed.
- Avoid hiking at dawn and dusk—the times mountain lions are most active.
- Watch for warning signs of mountain lion activity.
- Know how to behave if you encounter a mountain lion.

What to Do if You Encounter a Mountain Lion

In the vast majority of mountain lion encounters, these animals exhibit avoidance, indifference, or curiosity that never results in human injury. But it is natural to be alarmed if you have an encounter of any kind. Try to keep your cool and consider the following:

Recognize threatening mountain lion behavior. There are a few cues that may help you gauge the risk of attack. If a mountain lion is more than 50 yards away, and it directs its attention to you, it may be only curious. This situation represents

A tram platform on Rendezvous Mountain above Teton Village.

only a slight risk for adults, but a more serious risk to unaccompanied children. At this point you should move away, while keeping the animal in your peripheral vision. Also, look for rocks, sticks, or something to use as a weapon, just in case.

If a mountain lion is crouched and staring intensely at you less than 50 yards away, it may be assessing the chances of a successful attack. If this behavior continues, the risk of attack may be high.

Do not approach a mountain lion. Instead, give the animal the opportunity to move on. Slowly back away, but maintain eye contact if close. Mountain lions are not known to attack humans to defend young or a kill, but they have been reported to charge in rare instances and may want to stay in the area. It's best to choose another route or time to hike through the area.

Do not run from a mountain lion. Running may stimulate a predatory response.

Make noise. If you encounter a mountain lion, be vocal and talk or yell loudly and regularly. Try not to panic. Shout in a way that others in the area are aware of the situation.

Maintain eye contact. Eye contact presents a challenge to the mountain lion, showing you are aware of its presence. Eye contact also helps you know where it is. However, if the behavior of the mountain lion is not threatening (if it is, for example, grooming or periodically looking away), maintain visual contact through your peripheral vision and move away.

Appear larger than you are. Raise your arms above your head and make steady waving motions. Raise your jacket or another object above your head. Do not bend over, as this will make you appear smaller and more "preylike."

Grab the kids. If you are with small children, pick them up. First, bring children close to you, maintain eye contact with the mountain lion, and pull the children up without bending over. If you are with other children or adults, band together.

Defend yourself. If attacked, fight back. Try to remain standing. Do not feign death. Pick up a branch or rock; pull out a knife, pepper spray, or other deterrent

Heading down into Owel Creek from the Moose Basin Divide.

device. Remember that everything is a potential weapon, and individuals have fended off mountain lions with blows from rocks, tree limbs, and even cameras.

Defend others. Also, defend your hiking partners but don't defend your pet. In past attacks on children, adults have successfully stopped attacks. Cases involving pets are very dangerous and risky—physically defending a pet is not recommended.

Spread the word. Before leaving on your hike, discuss lions and teach others in your group how to behave in case of a mountain lion encounter. For example, anyone who starts running could bring on an attack.

Report encounters. If you have an encounter with a mountain lion, record your location and the details of the encounter, and notify the nearest landowner or land-managing agency. The land management agency (federal, state, or county) may want to visit the site and, if appropriate, post education/warning signs. Fish and wildlife agencies should also be notified because they record and track such encounters. If physical injury occurs, it is important to leave the area and not disturb the site of attack. Mountain lions that have attacked people must be killed, and an undisturbed site is critical for effectively locating the dangerous mountain lion.

Map Legend

—[62]—	U.S. highway
—(137)—	State highway
————	Paved road
= = = = =	Unpaved road
▬ ▬ ▬ ▬ ▬	Featured trail
- - - - - -	Other trail
•———•	Ski lift
✕	Bridge
♠	Cabin/lodge
⛺	Campground/campsite
≈	Falls
)(	Pass
▲	Peak
⊞	Picnic area
▪	Point of interest
🚶	Trailhead
❓	Visitor information
👁	View Point

Teton Village Area

1 Phelps Lake

Phelps Lake, a low-elevation lake, is one of the most popular destinations in the park. The short hike there is an easy day outing, but Phelps Lake is also an ideal place for the new backpacker to try that first night in the wilderness.

Phelps Lake is on the Valley Trail, which goes from Teton Village to the Lupine Meadows Trailhead. You can reach it from several trailheads, but the shortest, most popular route starts at the Death Canyon Trailhead (also called Whitegrass Trailhead on some maps and signs).

Start: Whitegrass/Death Canyon Trailhead.
Distance: 4.0 miles out and back.
Difficulty: Easy.
Seasons: July through September.

Maps: Earthwalk Press Grand Teton map; National Park Service handout map.
Trail contact: Grand Teton National Park, P.O. Drawer 170, Moose, WY 83012; (307) 739-3309; www.nps.gov/grte/.

Finding the trailhead: The trailhead is called Whitegrass on some maps and signs and Death Canyon on others, but it's the same place.

From Jackson, take Highway 22 west for about 6 miles to the Moose-Wilson Road junction just before the small town of Wilson. Turn right (north), go past Teton Village and into the park, and continue on this road (which turns to gravel) until you see the Death Canyon Trailhead turnoff on your left (west) 11.5 miles from Highway 22. From the north, the trailhead is 3.1 miles south of the Moose Visitor Center (see Locator Map) on Moose-Wilson Road, which turns south right across from the visitor center and doesn't go through the entrance station.

After turning off Moose-Wilson Road, drive 1.6 miles to the actual trailhead, the last mile of which is an unpaved road that can get rough. The park service recommends a high-clearance vehicle for this road. The trailhead has toilet facilities and a fairly large parking area, but this trailhead is so popular that it can be full, especially at midday.

The Hike

Only 0.1 mile after leaving the trailhead parking lot, you reach the first junction

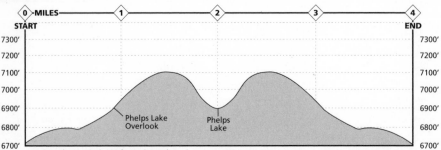

Intervals: Vertical, 100 ft; Horizontal, 1 mi.

Phelps Lake from the Phelps Lake Overlook.

with the Valley Trail. Go left (southwest) and hike 0.8 mile up a gradual hill to the Phelps Lake Overlook, where you get a nice view of the lake and the valley beyond.

From here, it's a steep downhill on switchbacks to Phelps Lake with a left (south) turn at the junction with the trail up Death Canyon. If you're camping, take a left on a spur trail just as you get to the lake instead of following the Valley Trail along the west side of the lake.

The well-maintained trail goes through mature forest most of the way with one brush-covered open slope above Phelps Lake. Watch for moose and black bears, which are commonly seen around Phelps Lake. Enjoy some fishing (with a Wyoming state fishing license) for brook, cutthroat, and lake trout. After your stay at Phelps Lake, retrace your steps back to the trailhead, keeping in mind that the way back involves a fairly steep climb up to the Phelps Lake Overlook.

Key Points

0.1 Junction with Valley Trail; turn left.
0.9 Phelps Lake Overlook.

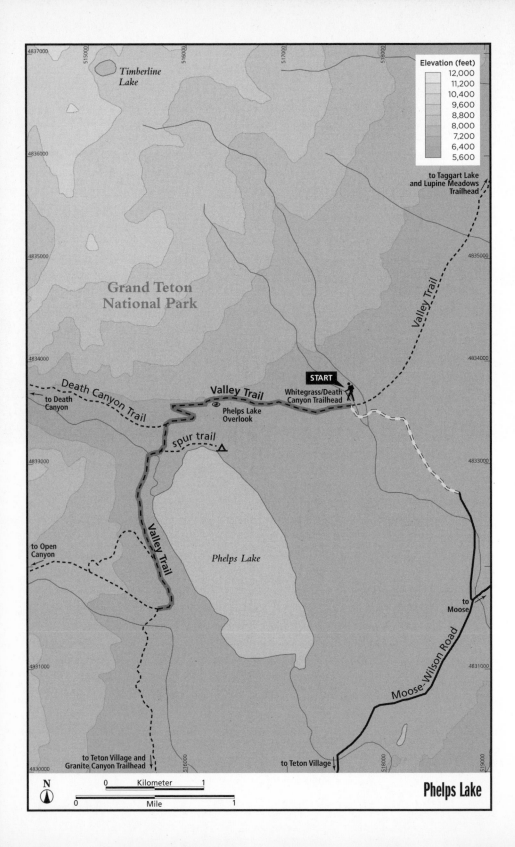

Phelps Lake

Camping at Phelps Lake.

1.6 Junction with Death Canyon Trail; turn left.
2.0 Phelps Lake.

Options: You can make this a shuttle by leaving a vehicle at the Granite Canyon Trailhead, which would make this a 6.1-mile hike.

Camping: Phelps Lake has three five-star designated campsites. As you approach the lake, watch for a junction with a trail going to the left (east) to the campsites. All campsites are on the north shore of the lake with a terrific view of the lake, fire pits, room for two tents, and a shared bear box. The campsites are out of sight of the main trail, but the three campsites are fairly close. Please talk softly to respect the privacy of others.

2 Marion Lake

Marion Lake is a long day hike, but you can start it the easy way, going downhill, if you take the aerial tram from Teton Village. Alternately, you could hike 6.6 miles up to the top of 10,450-foot Rendezvous Mountain on the tram service road. Obviously most people choose the tram, which leaves every fifteen minutes from 9:00 A.M. to 7:30 P.M. (there is a small fee to go up but no fee to go down). The Marion Lake hike also makes a nice two-day outing, with a pleasant overnight stay at one of the few mountain lakes in the park.

Start: Top of aerial tram at Teton Village.
Distance: 14.3-mile "lollipop" loop route.
Difficulty: Difficult day hike; moderate overnighter.
Seasons: July through September.

Maps: Earthwalk Press Grand Teton map; National Park Service handout map.
Trail contact: Grand Teton National Park, P.O. Drawer 170, Moose, WY 83012; (307) 739-3309; www.nps.gov/grte/.

Finding the trailhead: Take the aerial tram behind the main ski lodge in Teton Village to the top of Rendezvous Mountain to start this hike. Teton Village is 12.5 miles northwest of Jackson. From Jackson, take Highway 22 west of Jackson for about 6 miles to the Moose-Wilson Road junction just before the small town of Wilson. Turn right (north), go 6.5 miles, and turn left (west) into Teton Village. Park in the main ski lodge parking lot. Teton Village has restaurants, shopping, and toilet facilities in the lodge.

The Hike

Be sure to take a map on this hike. This route has an unusually high number of junctions, and it would be possible to get on the wrong trail without carefully following the map. In August and September, this route can be dry, as several intermittent streams dry up, so carry plenty of water. Horses are not allowed on the first 3.9 miles of this trail.

From the tram, hike down a steep ridgeline to the junction with the tram service road and the park boundary. Take this first leg of your trip slowly so you can soak in the incredible view of the Teton Range to the north—including Grand Teton peeping over the skyline—and the valley to the south.

At the park boundary, turn right and take one big switchback down the steep slope of Rendezvous Mountain into a bowl. You can see the trail heading up on the other side of the bowl. After the descent through some talus and subalpine vegetation, you move into spruce forest interspersed with large meadows. Most of the rest of the trail goes through this type of terrain.

When you get to the next junction at Middle Fork Cutoff Trail, you can take the loop in either direction, but this hike describes the clockwise route. Take a left

Coming back from Marion Lake.

at this junction and right at the next two junctions at the Teton Crest Trail (to Moose Creek Pass) and Game Creek, until you drop down into the North Fork of Granite Creek below Marion Lake. From there, you are treated with a short but steep climb up to the lake.

Marion Lake is a little jewel tucked in the shadow of mighty Housetop Mountain and surrounded by wildflower-carpeted meadows. Even if you aren't staying overnight, plan on spending some serious time at the lake. It's too nice to view quickly and then abandon. But don't take too long a nap. Unless you're spending the night, you have to make it back to the aerial tram before 7:30 P.M.

After a rest or lunch break or overnight stay at the lake, drop down into the South Fork, but this time turn left (east) down the North Fork of Granite Creek. Most of this leg of the trip goes through a giant meadow on the north side of the stream. At the junction with the Open Canyon Trail to the Mount Hunt Divide, veer right (east) through an open forest to the Rendezvous Mountain Trail. Turn right (south) and go through another huge meadow back to the Middle Fork Cutoff Trail junction you passed earlier in your trip.

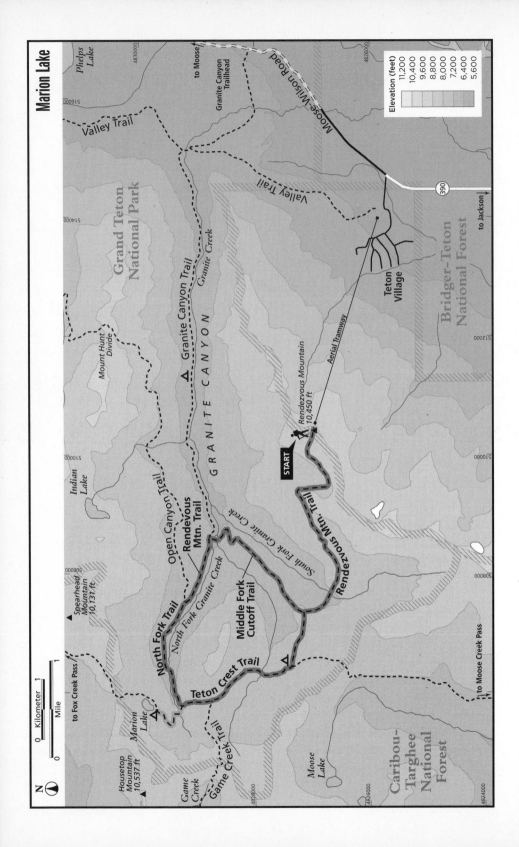

Marion Lake

From here, go left (east) and retrace your steps back to the aerial tram. Save some energy and water for the last pitch up to the tram. It can be a tough finish (especially on a hot day!) to a great hike.

Key Points

0.4 Junction with tram service road and park boundary; turn right.

3.9 Junction with Middle Fork Cutoff Trail; turn left.

4.4 Junction with Teton Crest Trail (to Moose Creek Pass); turn right.

5.4 Junction with Game Creek Trail; turn right.

6.0 Junction with North Fork Trail; turn left.

6.6 Marion Lake.

7.2 Junction with North Fork Trail; turn left.

8.4 Junction with Open Canyon Trail; turn right.

9.1 Junction with Rendezvous Mountain Trail; turn right.

10.8 Junction with Middle Fork Cutoff Trail; turn right.

13.9 Junction with tram service road; turn left.

14.3 Aerial tram.

Options: This hike can be taken in reverse, but you face a fairly steep climb coming out of the South Fork. You can also hike out and back and cut 1.5 miles off the total distance.

Side trip: If you have the time, you can hike about a half mile up from Marion Lake to a gorgeous high-altitude plateau. You can also take a side trip (about 1.4 miles round trip from Teton Crest Trail) over to Moose Creek Divide for a great view. The Game Creek Trail might look appealing, but it ends at the park boundary.

Camping: You have three choices. Marion Lake has three heavily used campsites with a good water source and nice views (although you can only see the lake from the first campsite and then just barely) with two raised tent pads each. You can also camp at the Middle Fork Camping Zone or the Upper Granite Canyon Camping Zone. Upper Granite has nicer campsites along the stream and good water sources.

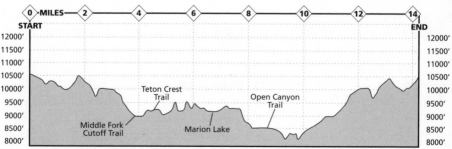

Intervals: Vertical, 500 ft; Horizontal, 2 mi.

The Middle Fork campsites generally offer better views, but water can be scarce in many areas, especially in late August and September when intermittent streams dry up. Marion Lake has designated campsites, but the two camping zones allow you to find your own campsite.

3 Rendezvous Mountain and Granite Canyon

This is the only hike in Grand Teton National Park that starts at the top of a mountain and goes to the valley floor, a perfect choice for hikers who don't like to climb hills. It makes a day hike or overnighter loop with a good shuttle option.

The trip actually starts in the valley floor at Teton Village at the aerial tramway to the top of Rendezvous Mountain. The tram starts running at 9:00 A.M. and runs about every fifteen minutes until 7:30 P.M. There is a small fee, but it's worth it. The only other option to get to the top of 10,450-foot Rendezvous Mountain is a 6.6-mile climb up the tram service road.

Start: Top of the Rendezvous Mountain aerial tram.
Distance: 12.8-mile loop.
Difficulty: Moderate.
Seasons: July and August.

Maps: Earthwalk Press Grand Teton map; National Park Service handout map.
Trail contact: Grand Teton National Park, P.O. Drawer 170, Moose, WY 83012; (307) 739-3309; www.nps.gov/grte/.

Finding the trailhead: Take the aerial tram behind the main ski lodge in Teton Village to the top of Rendezvous Mountain to start this hike. Teton Village is 12.5 miles northwest of Jackson. From Jackson, take Highway 22 west of Jackson for about 6 miles to the Moose-Wilson Road junction just before the small town of Wilson. Turn right (north), and go 6.5 miles. Turn left (west) into Teton Village. If you take the shuttle option, leave a vehicle or arrange to be picked up at the Granite Canyon Trailhead, which is 2.1 miles north of Teton Village on Moose-Wilson Road. Park in the main ski lodge parking lot. Teton Village has restaurants, shopping, and toilet facilities in the lodge.

The Hike

After getting off the tram, hike down the steep ridgeline to a junction with the tram service road at the park boundary. Take this first leg of your trip slowly so you can soak in the incredible view of the Teton Range to the north, including Grand Teton peeping over the skyline, and the valley to the south.

At the park boundary, turn right and take one big switchback down the steep slope of Rendezvous Mountain into a bowl. You can see the trail heading up on the other side of the bowl (the only hill you'll have to climb on this route). After the descent through some talus and subalpine vegetation, you move into spruce

Upper Granite Canyon.

forest interspersed with large meadows. Horses are not allowed on the first 3.9 miles of this trail.

Most of the rest of the trail goes through this type of terrain. In July and early August, expect a spectacular wildflower display in the meadows. In late August and September, this route can be dry, as several intermittent streams dry up, so carry plenty of water.

When you get to the Middle Fork Cutoff junction, go right (north), head through a giant meadow, and drop gradually down to Granite Creek. When you get to the stream, load up on water. Just past the stream is the junction with the Granite Canyon Trail. Go right (east) and start gradually dropping down to the valley floor. The trail stays close to the stream, mostly through meadows in the upper reaches, and becomes gradually more forested as you descend toward the valley floor. The canyon also narrows gradually as you descend. Don't be surprised to meet a group with horses in lower Granite Canyon.

When you reach the junction with the Valley Trail, go right (south) and cross the creek where you'll find another junction (only 0.1 mile down the trail). Go right

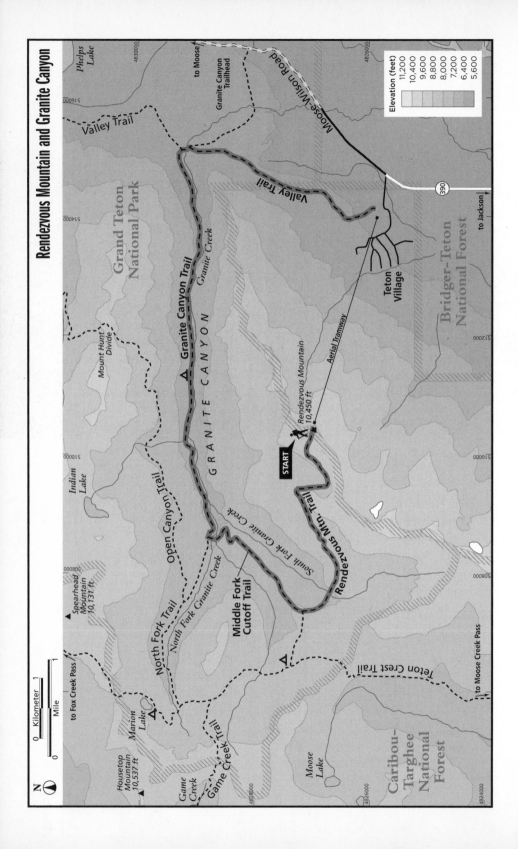

Rendezvous Mountain and Granite Canyon

N

Elevation (feet)

11,200
10,400
9,600
8,800
8,000
7,200
6,400
5,600

0   Kilometer   1

0   Mile   1

Phelps Lake

Valley Trail

to Moose

Granite Canyon Trailhead

Moose-Wilson Road

Grand Teton National Park

Granite Canyon Trail

Granite Creek

Valley Trail

390

to Jackson

Bridger-Teton National Forest

Mount Hunt Divide

GRANITE CANYON

Indian Lake

510000

Open Canyon Trail

Rendezvous Mountain 10,450 ft

Aerial Tramway

Teton Village

START

Rendezvous Mtn. Trail

South Fork Granite Creek

North Fork Trail

North Fork Granite Creek

Middle Fork Cutoff Trail

Spearhead Mountain 10,131 ft

Teton Crest Trail

to Moose Creek Pass

Caribou-Targhee National Forest

to Fox Creek Pass

Marion Lake

Housetop Mountain 10,537 ft

Game Creek Trail

Game Creek

Moose Lake

The trail below the tram on Rendezvous Mountain.

(south), and follow the Valley Trail to the park boundary and through the ski area back to the main lodge where the aerial tram begins. The trip through the ski area can get confusing, but focus on the aerial tram and you won't get off track.

Key Points

0.4 Park boundary and junction with tram service road; turn right.

3.9 Junction with Middle Fork Cutoff Trail; turn right.

5.6 Junction with Granite Canyon Trail; turn right.

10.3 Junction with Valley Trail; turn right.

10.4 Junction with trail to Granite Trailhead; turn right.

12.1 Park boundary.

12.8 Teton Village.

Options: You can make this hike with a convenient shuttle. Instead of turning right (south) at the Granite Canyon Trailhead junction, go left (east) and hike 1.5 miles to

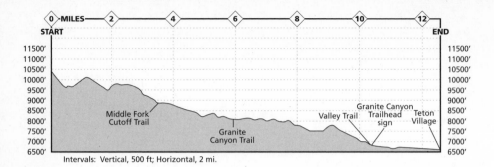

Intervals: Vertical, 500 ft; Horizontal, 2 mi.

the Granite Canyon Trailhead. This cuts about 0.9 mile off your trip. You can, of course, take this trip in reverse, but it would be uphill all the way.

Camping: You pass through two camping zones with undesignated campsites. The first, the Middle Fork Camping Zone, offers terrific campsites with good views, but water can be scarce later in the summer. The Lower Granite Camping Zone is mostly in the narrow portion of the canyon, and the best sites are close to the trail with limited privacy but close to the stream for easy access to water.

4 Death Canyon and the Mount Hunt Divide

This multiday trip through three canyons in the southern section of the park might not be viewed as a classic backpacking trip such as the Teton Crest or the Grand Teton Loop. It's shorter and lacks the popularity of other trips, but it has special appeal: Plan on seeing many fewer people on this trip, and with a side trip on the Death Canyon Shelf, you will see one of the better sections of the Teton Crest Trail.

Start: Whitegrass/Death Canyon Trailhead.
Distance: 24.2-mile loop.
Difficulty: Difficult.
Seasons: July and August.

Maps: Earthwalk Press Grand Teton map; National Park Service handout map.
Trail contact: Grand Teton National Park, P.O. Drawer 170, Moose, WY 83012; (307) 739–3309; www.nps.gov/grte/.

Finding the trailhead: The trailhead is called Whitegrass on some maps and signs and Death Canyon on others, but it's the same place.

From Jackson, take Highway 22 west of Jackson for about 6 miles to the Moose-Wilson Road junction just before the small town of Wilson. Turn right (north), go past Teton Village and into the park (no entrance station), and continue on this road (which turns to gravel) until you see the Death Canyon Trailhead turnoff on your left (west) 11.5 miles from Highway 22. From the north, the trailhead is 3.1 miles south of the Moose Visitor Center (see Locator Map) on

Hiking through Upper Death Canyon just below Fox Creek Pass.

Moose-Wilson Road, which turns south across from the visitor center and doesn't go through the entrance station.

After turning off Moose-Wilson Road, drive 1.6 miles to the actual trailhead, the last mile of which is an unpaved road that can get rough. The park service recommends a high-clearance vehicle for this road. The trailhead has toilet facilities and a fairly large parking area, but this trailhead is so popular that it can be full, especially at midday.

The Hike

Only 0.1 mile after leaving the trailhead parking lot, you reach the first junction with the Valley Trail. Go left (southwest) and hike 0.8 mile up a gradual hill to the Phelps Lake Overlook, where you get a nice view of the lake and the valley beyond. Phelps Lake is on the Valley Trail, which goes from Teton Village to the Lupine Meadows Trailhead. You can reach it from several trailheads, but the shortest, most popular route starts at the Death Canyon Trailhead (also called Whitegrass Trailhead on some maps and signs).

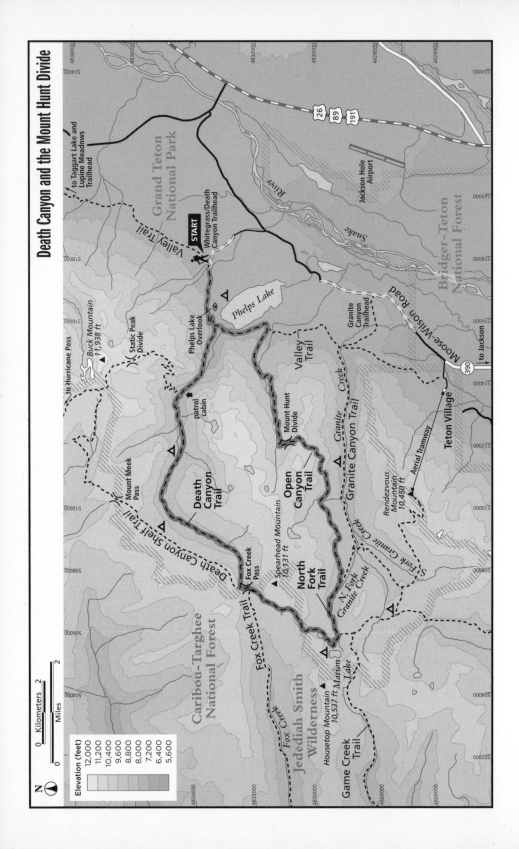

Death Canyon and the Mount Hunt Divide

From the overlook, it's a steep downhill on switchbacks to the junction with the Death Canyon Trail just above the lake. If you started late in the day and you're camping at Phelps Lake the first night out, take a left (east) on the Valley Trail, which goes by the lake, but if not, go right (west) and climb into Death Canyon.

The first part of the Death Canyon Trail to the patrol cabin at the junction with the Static Peak Divide Trail is a fairly serious hill. You climb most of the way on a slightly rocky trail along a classic mountain stream cascading out of Death Canyon, which is quite narrow and lined with cliffs most of the way. Like many of the canyons slicing into the Teton Range, the first part is the steepest. Turn around once or twice for a nice view of Phelps Lake and Jackson Hole.

At the patrol cabin, the trail levels out for a while and the stream turns smooth here and there. Then the trail gradually ascends all the way to Fox Creek Pass with 1 steep mile just before the pass. The switchbacks on the pass are short and functional, not those long, nearly level switchbacks that double the distance. Upper Death Canyon gets gradually more open and scenic as you near the pass. You hike in the shadow of the Death Canyon Shelf to the northwest.

At Fox Creek Pass, you leave the park and enter the Jedediah Smith Wilderness in the Targhee National Forest. Go left (south) at the junction with the trail up the Death Canyon Shelf at the pass. In only 0.1 mile, you hit a somewhat confusing junction (no sign when I was there) with the trail dropping down Fox Creek to the west. Watch the map, and be sure to go left (south), and hike along a mostly level plateau for about 2 miles over to Marion Lake. This is a very scenic leg of the hike with massive Housetop Mountain ahead and extremely well-named Spearhead Mountain to the left. When you enter the park again 0.4 mile above Marion Lake, you hike down a steep hill to Marion Lake, a small, jewel-like mountain lake you can see all the way down the ridge.

After a stay at Marion Lake, continue steeply downhill for another 0.6 mile until you get to the North Fork of Granite Creek. At the creek bottom, take a left (east) at the junction with the trail going to the South Fork of Granite Creek and to Teton Village. Hike 3.4 miles through the mostly open terrain along the north side of the creek until you reach the Open Canyon Trail to the Mount Hunt Divide.

Go left (northeast), and start hiking the most difficult leg of the trip. The next 4.1 miles go by slowly, as you steadily climb right from the junction up to the Mount Hunt Divide. This tough climb gains about 1,600 feet, and seems long. The terrain fools you, as you think you're "almost there," but it takes much longer than expected. For much of the way, the trail traverses a scenic contour above Granite Canyon.

Mount Hunt Divide (when you finally get there!) offers some spectacular views of the southern Teton Range. You can see Rendezvous Mountain and Apres Vous Peak, which provide the slopes for the Teton Village Ski Area, to the south and most of the big peaks of the Teton Range to the north.

From the divide, the trail drops precipitously down into (not so) Open Canyon. You drop into whitebark pine and keep going down until you get to a mature lodgepole forest, switchbacking all the way to the creek bottom. Once at the bottom, the trail becomes mostly level as it follows the stream grade down to the Valley Trail. Watch for moose.

Go left (east) at the cutoff trail just before you reach the Valley Trail, and left (north) again when you get to the Valley Trail 0.8 mile later. Shortly after getting on the Valley Trail, start hiking the west shore of expansive Phelps Lake. If you plan to camp at the lake, watch for the spur trail to the right, which takes you around to the campsites on the north shore. Watch for moose and black bears, which are commonly seen around Phelps Lake. After your stay at the lake, retrace your steps to the trailhead, keeping in mind that the way back involves a fairly steep climb up to the Phelps Lake Overlook.

Key Points

0.1 Junction with Valley Trail; turn left.

0.9 Phelps Lake Overlook.

1.6 Junction with Death Canyon Trail; turn right.

3.7 Patrol cabin and junction with trail to Static Peak Divide; turn left.

9.2 Fox Creek Pass and park boundary.

9.2 Junction with Death Canyon Shelf Trail; turn left.

9.3 Junction with Fox Creek Trail; turn left.

11.1 Park boundary.

11.5 Marion Lake.

12.1 Junction with North Fork Trail; turn left.

13.3 Junction with Open Canyon Trail; turn left.

17.4 Mount Hunt Divide.

20.8 Junction with cutoff trail to Granite Canyon; turn left.

21.6 Junction with Valley Trail; turn left.

22.2 Phelps Lake.

22.6 Junction with Death Canyon Trail; turn right.

23.3 Phelps Lake Overlook.

24.1 Junction with Death Canyon Trailhead Trail; turn right.

24.2 Whitegrass/Death Canyon Trailhead.

Suggested itinerary:
First night: Lower Death Canyon.
Second night: Marion Lake.
Third night: Phelps Lake.

Options: Add a day to the trip by spending a sure-to-always-be-remembered night on Death Canyon Shelf. If you're interested in this option, turn right (northeast) at Fox Creek Pass and hike 2 to 3 miles along the shelf until you find a five-star campsite (which won't be difficult) and settle in for a great night in the high country. In the morning, head over to Marion Lake to your next campsite.

You could, of course, do this trip in reverse, but the Mount Hunt Divide is a monster hill from either side.

Side trip: You would really miss something if you didn't take the side trip out and back on the Death Canyon Shelf—or even better, spend the night.

Camping: This is a difficult trip to plan because the Open Canyon and Mount Hunt Camping Zones are probably the least desirable in the park. Having a great campsite is important to me, which is why I recommend doing the 11 tough miles from Marion Lake to Phelps Lake. I camped in the Open Canyon Camping Zone on the east side of the divide, which cut the day's backpack down to 7 or 8 miles. However, I was unhappy with the camping choices in this zone. Ditto for the Mount Hunt Camping Zone I hiked through earlier in the day. Earlier in the year, I had been pleasantly surprised with how much I enjoyed a night at Phelps Lake, so if I did this trip again I'd roll out early from Marion Lake and go all the way to Phelps Lake. You could actually hike all the way out to the trailhead, but this would be almost 13 miles with a big hill—and you'd miss a nice camping experience at Phelps Lake.

The Death Canyon Camping Zone is delightful with its many five-star campsites, especially in the upper reaches, good access to water, and nice views of the Death Canyon Shelf or Fox Creek Pass. This is an undesignated camping area, so find a site with a nice view and set up a no-trace camp.

If you spend a night on the shelf, arrange for some good weather because it could be ugly on this high, exposed bench. In August and September, water can get scarce on the shelf, especially in the southern part.

Marion Lake has three designated campsites with two tent pads each. The view is not that spectacular, but it's an easy walk to get water. The sites are about 200 feet from the main trail but fairly close together with limited privacy.

Both the Mount Hunt and Open Canyon Camping Zones offer a poor choice of good campsites, and it's quite difficult to find water late in the season. One basic problem is finding a tent site that's anywhere near level.

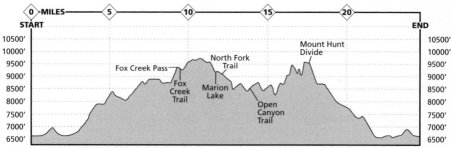

Intervals: Vertical, 500 ft; Horizontal, 5 mi.

Phelps Lake has three five-star designated campsites. As you approach the lake, watch for a junction with a trail going to the right (north) to the campsites. All of them are on the north shore of the lake with terrific views of the lake, fire pits, room for two tents, and a shared bear box. The campsites are out of sight of the main trail, but the three campsites are fairly close, so please talk softly to respect the privacy of others.

5 The Teton Crest

It really doesn't get any better than this. A truly spectacular multiday adventure starting from a 10,450 feet elevation. The Teton Crest is a long (at least three nights) shuttle backpacking trip. This trip has the incredible luxury of starting at 10,450 feet and ending at 6,875 feet, a net loss of 3,575. That's not to say, however, that there is no hill climbing. Quite to the contrary, you get to sweat your way up three big hills, including the two most famous in the park—Hurricane Pass and Paintbrush Divide. And, of course, you go by the three most famous high-country lakes—Marion Lake, Lake Solitude, and Holly Lake. Lastly, you get the best mountain scenery possible, including several miles in the shadow of the Grand Teton.

What more could you want? Well, you want good weather, a week off, and the advanced physical conditioning necessary to enjoy it.

Start: Top of aerial tram at Teton Village.
Distance: 35.4-mile shuttle.
Difficulty: Difficult.
Seasons: Late July through mid-September.

Maps: Earthwalk Press Grand Teton map; National Park Service handout map.
Trail contact: Grand Teton National Park, P.O. Drawer 170, Moose, WY 83012; (307) 739–3309; www.nps.gov/grte/.

Finding the trailhead: For the shuttle, leave a vehicle at the Leigh Lake Trailhead at the String Lake Picnic Area. To find this trailhead, take U.S. Highway 89 north of Jackson for 11.5 miles and turn left (west) at the Moose Junction. Drive past the Moose Visitor Center (see Locator Map) and through the entrance station (about a mile after turning off the highway). Follow this paved park road for another 9.7 miles from the entrance station to the Jenny Lake turnoff. Turn left (west) and drive 0.6 mile (follow the signs and take two right turns) to the String Lake Trailhead and 0.3 mile farther to the String Lake Picnic Area. The Leigh Lake Trailhead is in the northwest corner of the picnic area. From the north, drive 9.9 miles from the Jackson Lake Junction and turn right (west) at the Jenny Lake turnoff. There are toilet facilities in the picnic area at the Leigh Lake Trailhead.

To start the hike, take the aerial tramway behind the main ski lodge in Teton Village to the top of Rendezvous Mountain. Teton Village is 12.5 miles northwest of Jackson. From Jackson, take Highway 22 west of Jackson for about 6 miles to the Moose-Wilson Road junction just before the small town of Wilson. Turn right (north), and go 6.5 miles, and turn left (west) into Teton Village. Park in the main ski lodge parking lot.

Grand Teton from Rendezvous Mountain.

The Hike

There aren't many hikes that start out downhill, but if you take the aerial tram from Teton Village, this can be one of them. As you stand at the main ski lodge in Teton Village, you have a tough choice. You can carry your backpack stuffed with six days of food and gas up 4,100 feet over 6.6 miles of constantly switchbacking service road or you can ride up the tram in ten minutes without breaking a sweat. Think about it!

Obviously, most people choose the tram, which leaves every fifteen minutes from 9:00 A.M. to 7:30 P.M. There is a small fee. Be sure to keep your map out. This route has an unusually high number of junctions, and without carefully following the map it is possible to get on the wrong trail.

From the tram, hike down a steep ridgeline to the junction with the tram service road and the park boundary. Take this first leg of your trip slowly so you can soak in the incredible view of the Teton Range to the north, including Grand Teton peeping over the skyline (you'll be on the other side of it three days later), and the valley to the south.

Catching our breath and enjoying the scenery of Hurricane Pass.

At the park boundary, turn right and take one big switchback down the steep slope of Rendezvous Mountain into a bowl. You can see the trail heading up on the other side of the bowl. After the descent through some talus and subalpine vegetation, you move into spruce forest interspersed with large meadows. You hike through this type of terrain until Marion Lake, where you climb up to the alpine country along the Teton Crest Trail. In August and September, this route can be dry, as several intermittent streams dry up, so carry plenty of water. Horses are not allowed on the first 3.9 miles of this trail.

When you get to the next junction, take a left (northeast) and a right (north) at the next two junctions to Moose Creek Pass and Game Creek, until you drop down into the North Fork of Granite Creek below Marion Lake. There you are treated with a short but steep climb up to the lake.

Marion Lake is a little jewel tucked in the shadow of mighty Housetop Mountain and surrounded by wildflower-carpeted meadows. Even if you aren't camping here, plan on spending some serious time at the lake. It's too nice to quickly view and then abandon, so it makes a good spot for the first night out.

After you stay at Marion Lake, you face a 0.4-mile hill up to the park boundary and an unnamed divide on the flanks of Housetop Mountain. Then to Fox Creek Pass it's mostly level, alpine hiking with great views all around, especially of aptly named Spearhead Mountain off to the right (east).

Just before reaching Fox Creek Pass, a confusing junction (no sign when we were there) with a trail head off to the left (west) down Fox Creek into the Jedediah Smith Wilderness. Turn right (north). Just over a small hill you'll see Fox Creek Pass and the park boundary. At the pass, you can go either right (northeast) down Death Canyon or left (north) and continue along the Teton Crest Trail on Death Canyon Shelf.

The next 11 miles—to Fox Creek Pass, along Death Canyon Shelf, over Mount Meek Divide, through Alaska Basin, and up to Hurricane Pass—are the absolute essence of the Teton Range, the choicest of the choice for mountain scenery. Even though I have been backpacking for thirty-five years, this is a truly memorable stretch of trail, and I'm sure it will be for you, too.

Death Canyon Shelf is a flat bench on the east flanks of a series of awesome peaks—Fossil Mountain, Bannon Peak, Mount Jedediah Smith, and Mount Meek. To the east, you can look down Death Canyon all the way to Jackson Hole in the distance. The shelf is a great choice for the second night out. It's exposed to weather, though, so be prepared, and water can be hard to find in September.

From Mount Meek Divide, you drop down into gorgeous Alaska Basin. Several small lakes dot the basin, and there is a labyrinth of trails. All are distinct and well signed, however, so you should not have a problem finding your way past Basin Lakes and Sunset Lake and up to Hurricane Pass. A hurricane-force wind was blowing when I was there, and I suspect this is a common occurrence.

From the pass you can see it all, including Grand Teton (and Middle and South Teton), Mount Moran to the north, and, right below you, Schoolroom Glacier. Unless the weather prohibits a long stay (as it did when I was there), spend some quality time on Hurricane Pass identifying all the peaks.

The trip from Marion Lake to Hurricane Pass might have been the best ever, but the section between the pass and Holly Lake rivals it for scenic beauty. The trail down Hurricane Pass is steep right at the top but soon becomes a nicely switch-backed trail. If you have some extra time, set up camp near the top of the South Fork Cascade Camping Zone and take a side trip up toward Avalanche Divide for a close-up view of the three Tetons.

After a night along the South Fork of Cascade Creek, drop down to the junction with the main trail up Cascade Canyon. You could bail out at this point and go down to the west-shore boat dock on Jenny Lake, but if you do you miss Lake Solitude and the Paintbrush Divide, so go left (northwest) at this junction.

The trail up the North Fork of Cascade Creek is forested at first but soon breaks out into subalpine meadows and a virtual kaleidoscope of wildflowers. It's 2.7 miles to Lake Solitude, but you probably want to set up your fourth camp somewhere near

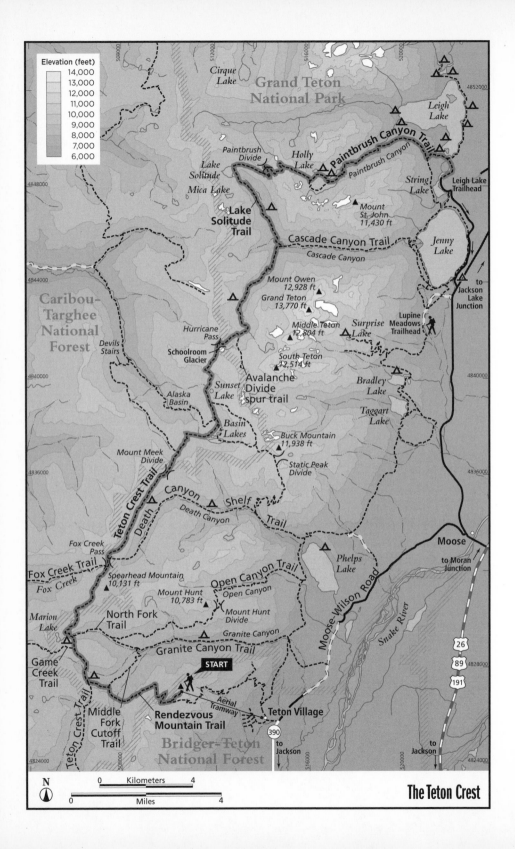

The Teton Crest

the top of the North Fork Cascade Camping Zone. So, it will only be a short walk up to Lake Solitude after camp has been set up. Lake Solitude is remote but sometimes not as quiet as it used to be. It's now a popular destination, so expect to see other hikers in the area during the day.

After the fourth night below Lake Solitude, psych yourself up for the biggest hill of the trip, the 2.4 miles up to 10,700-foot Paintbrush Divide. The trail is in great shape, and when you stop to rest, you have some great scenery to enjoy—Lake Solitude and Mica Lake below and Grand Teton to the southeast.

Paintbrush Divide is not quite as awesome as Hurricane Pass, but it's a very close second. After soaking up the scenery for a while, start down the divide into Paintbrush Canyon on one big switchback through a talus slope and, even in September, over some snowbanks clinging to this north-facing slope. In fact, it's dangerous to try this slope without an ice axe until August on many years. Before you leave on this trip, be sure to quiz a ranger on the snow conditions on Paintbrush Divide. If an ice axe is recommended, be sure you know how to use it to rescue yourself if you fall. If this is beyond your capabilities, delay this trip until snow conditions improve.

If you're doing a five-night trip, plan on Holly Lake for your last night in paradise. The junction is only 1.3 miles from the divide, but it's another 0.3 mile uphill to the lake and about that far over to the campsites on the east end of the cirque containing Holly Lake.

After your stay at Holly Lake, follow the rest of the cutoff trail left (east) from the lake. Rejoin the main trail down Paintbrush Canyon 0.4 mile from the lake and gradually drop out of the high country into the mature forest of the low country.

When you get to the junction with the String Lake Trail, go left (east) and hike a mere 0.7 mile to the bridge over the short stream between String Lake and Leigh Lake. Cross the bridge to the junction with the Leigh Lake Trail just on the other side of the bridge, turn right (south), and hike a super-flat 0.8 mile along String Lake back to the Leigh Lake Trailhead and String Lake Picnic Area parking lot, where you are likely to feel somewhat reluctant to end a truly remarkable backpacking trip.

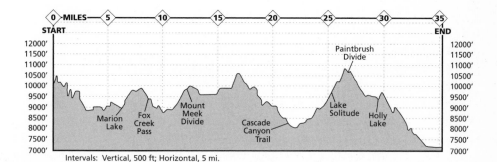

Intervals: Vertical, 500 ft; Horizontal, 5 mi.

Hiking on the Paintbrush Divide in September.

Key Points

0.4 Junction with tram service road and park boundary.

3.9 Junction with Middle Fork Cutoff Trail.

4.4 Junction with Teton Crest Trail.

5.4 Junction with Game Creek Trail.

6.0 Junction with North Fork Trail.

6.6 Marion Lake.

7.0 Park boundary.

8.8 Junction with trail down Fox Creek.

8.9 Fox Creek Pass and junction with Death Canyon Shelf Trail.

12.4 Mount Meek Divide and park boundary.

12.6 Junction with trail to Devils Stairs.

14.4 Basin Lakes.

14.6 Junction with trail to Buck Mountain Pass.

15.4 Junction with second trail to Buck Mountain Pass.

15.7 Sunset Lake.

17.4 Hurricane Pass and Schoolroom Glacier.

19.0 Junction with trail to Avalanche Pass.

22.5 Junction with Cascade Canyon Trail.

25.2 Lake Solitude.

27.6 Paintbrush Divide.

28.9 Junction with spur trail to Holly Lake.

29.2 Holly Lake.

29.7 Return to main trail in Paintbrush Canyon.

33.9 Junction with String Lake Trail.

34.6 Junction with Leigh Lake Trail.

35.4 Leigh Lake Trailhead and String Lake Picnic Area.

Suggested itinerary:

First night: Marion Lake.
Second night: Death Canyon Shelf.
Third night: South Fork Cascade Canyon.
Fourth night: North Fork Cascade Canyon.
Fifth night: Holly Lake.

Options: This hike can be taken in reverse, but you face more climbing because at the end you will need to get up Rendezvous Mountain on foot. You can bail out and make the trip shorter by coming down Death Canyon or Cascade Canyon.

Side trip: If you have the time and energy (and enough granola bars!), try the side trips up to the Static Peak Divide and the Avalanche Divide.

Camping: For the first night out, you have four choices. Marion Lake has three heavily used campsites and a good water source, nice views (although you can only see the lake from the first campsite and then just barely), and two raised tent pads each. Marion Lake may be the best choice for the first night out because it's nicely located at 6.6 miles from the aerial tram. Although not as convenient, you can also camp at the Middle Fork Camping Zone or the Upper Granite Canyon Camping Zone. Upper Granite has nicer campsites along the stream with good water sources. The Middle Fork campsites generally offer better views, but water can be scarce in many areas, especially in late August and September when intermittent streams dry up. Marion Lake has designated campsites, but the two camping zones allow you to find your own campsite. For the fourth choice, you can hike past Marion Lake and camp outside the park.

For the second night, you probably want to strive for the Death Canyon Shelf and the open camping zone with no designated campsites. Water is scarce on the south part of the shelf but adequately abundant from the midpoint on. The scenery

Jackson Hole from the Teton Village aerial tramway.

from camp will be the best possible. There's enough room to find privacy, and rest assured that the air-conditioning will be on.

If you're trying to cover this route with four nights out, hike past the shelf and camp anywhere in Alaska Basin. This is outside the park, so National Park Service regulations don't apply. However, be sure to walk softly and set up a no-trace camp in this fragile highland.

For the next night out, you can opt for either the South Fork Cascade or North Fork Cascade Camping Zones. Both areas have indicated sites, but you can camp anywhere in these areas. The indicated sites are nicely set up, however, so we can't imagine wanting to find something new. All of these campsites (and there are plenty) are good. You won't be disappointed. The main issue is how far you want to go that day. The camping in the North Fork is probably even nicer than in the South Fork because most sites come with a stunning view of Grand Teton.

Holly Lake has three designated campsites about a quarter mile from the lake at the end of a trail that crosses the outlet on rocks and goes up on a slope above the lake. Campsite 3 is the most private. Surprisingly, the campsites do not have good views right from camp. Water is fairly accessible from all three sites, which have two tent pads each and share a bear box.

The Lower Paintbrush Canyon Camping Zone has nine indicated campsites strategically located on high points above the trail. (See the Introduction, Using This FalconGuide, for an explanation of indicated campsites.) Most of them are private (about 100 yards from the trail) but have only one tent pad (the park service plans to add more later). Some of them have a fairly long hike to water. Most of the camp-sites are five-star with a good view.

You can also camp in the Upper Paintbrush Camping Zone along the main trail below Holly Lake. This zone requires a camping permit different from the one for Holly Lake even though they are not far apart.

Jenny Lake Area

6 Leigh Lake

Although Leigh Lake is also a nice hike in July, August, and September, it's a great choice for May or June. The snow leaves this area much sooner than the high country. The scenery is unbeatable with Mount Moran and Rockchuck Peak looming above Leigh Lake and narrow Paintbrush and Leigh Canyons slicing into the Teton Range above the west shore on each side of Mount Woodring, the high peak between Mount Moran and Rockchuck Peak.

This is a short, flat hike along the shoreline of two lakes. The trail is in terrific shape (often double wide) all the way, and sandy beaches provide inviting rest spots along both String Lake and Leigh Lake. In addition to being one of the best day hikes in the park, Leigh Lake also provides a wonderful choice for an easy overnighter, ideal for the beginning backpacker or a family with children wanting to experience that first overnight stay in the wilderness.

Start: Leigh Lake Trailhead at the String Lake Picnic Area.
Distance: 5.4 miles out and back.
Difficulty: Easy.
Seasons: July through September.

Maps: Earthwalk Press Grand Teton map; National Park Service handout map.
Trail contact: Grand Teton National Park, P.O. Drawer 170, Moose, WY 83012; (307) 739-3309; www.nps.gov/grte/.

Finding the trailhead: Take U.S. Highway 89 north of Jackson for 11.5 miles and turn left (west) at Moose Junction. Drive past the Moose Visitor Center (see Locator Map) and through the entrance station (about a mile after turning off the highway). Follow this paved park road for another 9.7 miles from the entrance station to the Jenny Lake turnoff. Turn left here and drive 0.6 mile (follow the signs and take two right turns) to the String Lake Trailhead and, 0.3 mile farther, the String Lake Picnic Area. The Leigh Lake Trailhead is in the northwest corner of the picnic area. From the north, drive 9.9 miles from the Jackson Lake Junction and turn right (west) at the Jenny Lake turnoff. Park in the large parking lot at the picnic area. There are toilet facilities in the picnic area at the Leigh Lake Trailhead.

The Hike

Halfway along String Lake, you'll see a horse trail coming in from the right (east). From this point on, don't be surprised to see a string of horses with park visitors getting their first horse-riding experience. At the end of String Lake; go right (north) at the junction, where you'll see a portage trail for people hauling their canoes up to Leigh Lake. The foot trail angles off to the right of the portage trail.

After a short 0.2-mile walk through lodgepole pines, you get your first view of enormous Leigh Lake, a 250-foot-deep basin formed by the glaciers that once flowed out of Leigh and Paintbrush Canyons. The trail goes along the shoreline, and Mount Moran provides the scenic backdrop.

Wading on one of the sandy beaches along the east shore of Leigh Lake.

About halfway along Leigh Lake, you pass by the east-shore campsites complete with sandy beaches and world-record vistas. The end of the lake is about three-tenths of a mile past the campsites. You can turn around at the campsites or the end of the lake.

Key Points

0.4 Horse trail comes in from the east.

0.8 End of String Lake and junction with trail to Holly Lake; turn right.

1.0 Leigh Lake.

2.4 East-shore campsites.

2.7 End of Leigh Lake.

Options: If you don't want to retrace your steps all the way back; turn right (west) at the junction at the end of String Lake and take the String Lake Trail back to the picnic area. This adds 2.5 miles to your hike.

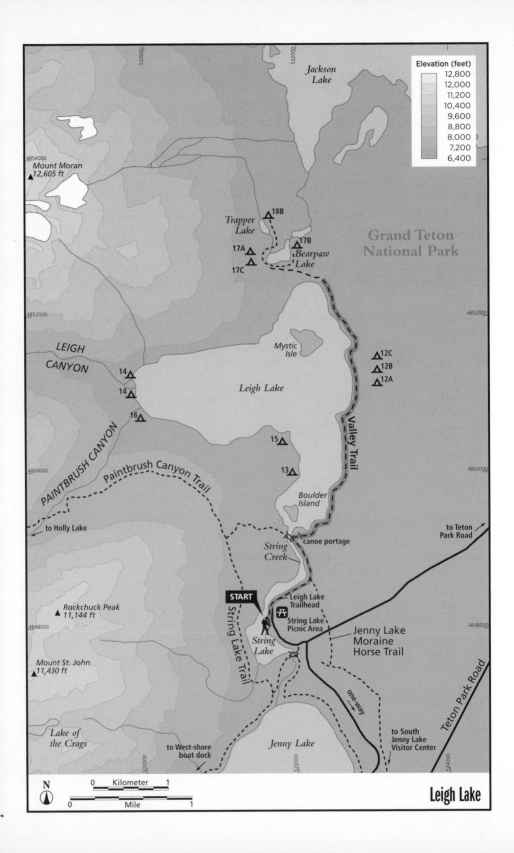

Elevation (feet)
12,800
12,000
11,200
10,400
9,600
8,800
8,000
7,200
6,400

Jackson Lake

Trapper Lake

18B
17B
17A
Bearpaw Lake
17C

Grand Teton National Park

▲ Mount Moran
12,605 ft

Mystic Isle

LEIGH CANYON

14
14
16

Leigh Lake

12C
12B
12A

Valley Trail

15

13

PAINTBRUSH CANYON

Paintbrush Canyon Trail

← to Holly Lake

Boulder Island

canoe portage

String Creek

to Teton → Park Road

START

Leigh Lake Trailhead

▲ Rockchuck Peak
11,144 ft

String Lake Trail

String Lake Picnic Area

Jenny Lake Moraine Horse Trail

▲ Mount St. John
11,430 ft

String Lake

one-way

Lake of the Crags

to South Jenny Lake Visitor Center

Teton Park Road

Jenny Lake

to West-shore boat dock

N

0   Kilometer   1

0   Mile   1

Leigh Lake

Side trip: If you need more hiking, hike up to Bearpaw Lake, which adds 2.4 miles to the total distance. Add another 0.8 mile by going up to Trapper Lake.

Camping: The campsites on the east shore of Leigh Lake are extraordinarily nice and definitely get a five-star rating. You get a spectacular view of Mount Moran and the Teton Range right from the food areas. Each campsite has a fire pit, two or three good tent sites, and a bear box for storing food at night. Since the three campsites are on the lakeshore, water is readily accessible. There are three campsites, but the first one is the group site. The only knock on these sites is that the trail goes right by them, sacrificing privacy. However, you would not want to miss the scenery from the trail by routing it away from the lakes to miss the campsites.

7 Bradley Lake

Bradley Lake, like Taggart Lake, was named for a member of the 1872 Hayden Expedition and, also like Taggart Lake, is one of the most accessible and popular short day hikes in the park.

Start: Taggart Lake Trailhead.
Distance: 5.3-mile "lollipop" loop.
Difficulty: Easy.
Seasons: July through September.
Maps: Earthwalk Press Grand Teton map;

National Park Service trail guide to Taggart and Bradley lakes.
Trail contact: Grand Teton National Park, P.O. Drawer 170, Moose, WY 83012; (307) 739-3309; www.nps.gov/grte/.

Finding the trailhead: Take U.S. Highway 89 north of Jackson for 11.5 miles and turn left (west) at the Moose Junction. Drive past the Moose Visitor Center (see Locator Map) and through the entrance station (about a mile after turning off the highway). Follow this paved park road for another 2.2 miles from the entrance station and turn left (west) to the Taggart Lake Trailhead parking lot. From the north, drive 17.4 miles from the Jackson Lake Junction and turn right (west) into the trailhead parking lot. This trailhead has toilet facilities and plenty of parking.

The Hike

The first 0.2 mile of the trail to the first junction, is double wide and flat and goes through a sagebrush-dotted meadow. At the junction; go right (northwest) and the trail becomes singletrack and goes past some minor development and onto Taggart Creek, which you cross on a sturdy footbridge. The trail then climbs gradually up to the top of a moraine where you get constantly good views of the Teton Range, including Grand Teton. This section of the trail also goes through a 1996 forest-fire burn, so you can observe how the forest regenerates itself.

You reach the Bradley Lake Trail 1.3 miles from the trailhead. Turn right (north) and continue through another mile of the same terrain to 7,022-foot Bradley Lake,

Bradley and Taggart lakes viewed from the trail to Surprise Lake and Garnet Canyon.

a deep pool at the foot of Garnet Canyon, impounded there long ago when the gla-cier flowing out of the canyon melted.

You can retrace your steps to the trailhead, but it only adds 0.7 mile to make a loop and see two lakes instead of one. If you prefer the loop option, take a left (south) on the Valley Trail, which connects Bradley and Taggart lakes, and climb over a short but steep ridge (actually another moraine) between the lakes.

It's only 1.1 miles to forest-lined Taggart Lake, which is slightly lower in eleva-tion (6,902 feet) but otherwise similar to Bradley Lake. I like the view from Taggart better than from Bradley, but they are both beautiful mountain lakes.

Before you reach the footbridge over the outlet of Taggart Lake; turn left (east) on the Taggart Lake Trail and follow it for 0.5 mile back to the junction with the Bradley Lake Trail. Retrace your steps back to the trailhead.

Key Points

0.2 Start of loop trail; turn right.

0.7 Taggart Creek.

1.3 Junction with Bradley Lake Trail; turn right.

2.2 Bradley Lake and junction with Valley Trail; turn left.

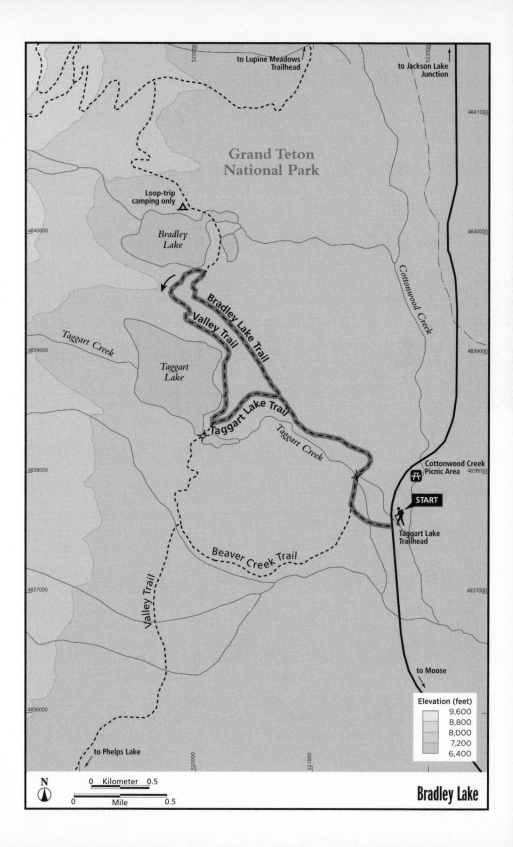

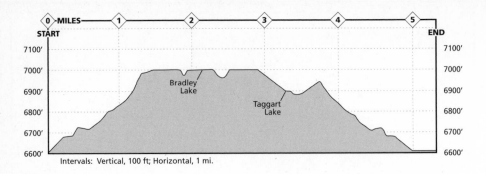

Intervals: Vertical, 100 ft; Horizontal, 1 mi.

3.3 Taggart Lake and junction with Taggart Lake Trail; turn left.

4.0 Junction with Bradley Lake Trail; turn left.

5.1 Junction with loop trail; turn left.

5.3 Taggart Lake Trailhead.

Options: You can take the loop in either direction with no increase in difficulty. You can also take the out-and-back option, and you can add another 0.8 mile to the hike by following the Valley Trail south past Taggart Lake to the junction with the Beaver Creek Trail. Turn left (east) at the junction and follow this trail back to the Taggart Lake Trailhead. This option makes a true loop out of this trip.

Camping: There is a designated campsite at Bradley Lake, but it is reserved for backpackers taking the Grand Teton Loop.

8 Moose Ponds

Moose Ponds is a short loop day hike for wildlife watchers. The area around South Jenny Lake is heavily developed—and a bit confusing to the first-time visitor. Fortunately, if necessary, you can get your questions answered in the visitor center.

Start: South Jenny Lake Visitor Center.
Distance: 2.6-mile loop.
Difficulty: Easy.
Seasons: July through September.

Maps: Earthwalk Press Grand Teton map; National Park Service handout map.
Trail contact: Grand Teton National Park, P.O. Drawer 170, Moose, WY 83012; (307) 739-3309; www.nps.gov/grte/.

Finding the trailhead: Take U.S. Highway 89 north of Jackson for 11.5 miles and turn left (west) at the Moose Junction. Drive past the Moose Visitor Center (see Locator Map) and through the entrance station (about a mile after turning off the highway). Follow this paved park

Moose Ponds overlook. ▶

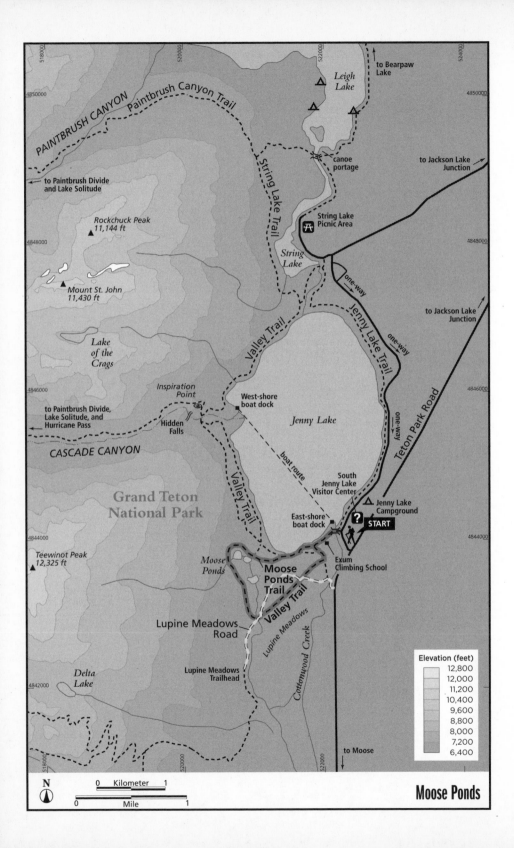

PAINTBRUSH CANYON

Paintbrush Canyon Trail

to Paintbrush Divide
and Lake Solitude

Rockchuck Peak
11,144 ft

▲ Mount St. John
11,430 ft

Lake
of the
Crags

to Paintbrush Divide,
Lake Solitude, and
Hurricane Pass

Inspiration
Point

Hidden
Falls

CASCADE CANYON

Grand Teton
National Park

Teewinot Peak
12,325 ft ▲

Moose
Ponds

Moose
Ponds
Trail

Lupine Meadows
Road

Delta
Lake

Lupine Meadows
Trailhead

Leigh
Lake

to Bearpaw
Lake

canoe
portage

to Jackson Lake
Junction

String Lake Trail

String Lake
Picnic Area

String
Lake

one-way

Jenny Lake Trail

to Jackson Lake
Junction

Valley Trail

one-way

Jenny Lake

boat route

West-shore
boat dock

one-way

South
Jenny Lake
Visitor Center

Teton Park Road

East-shore
boat dock

? ▲ Jenny Lake
Campground

START

Exum
Climbing School

Valley Trail

Lupine Meadows

Cottonwood Creek

to Moose

N

0   Kilometer   1

0   Mile   1

Elevation (feet)

	12,800
	12,000
	11,200
	10,400
	9,600
	8,800
	8,000
	7,200
	6,400

Moose Ponds

road for another 6.8 miles from the entrance station to the South Jenny Lake turnoff. Turn left (west) and drive less than a half mile to the visitor center. From the north, drive 12.8 miles from the Jackson Lake Junction and turn right (west) at the South Jenny Lake turnoff.

The South Jenny Lake area has a general store, visitor center, boat dock, toilet facilities, and, usually, plenty of room to park. This is a heavily used area, and the boat ride across the lake is very popular, so in midday during the summer the parking lot can be full.

The Hike

From the visitor center, start following the trail around the south edge of the lake. You immediately cross over Cottonwood Creek (outlet to Jenny Lake), along the north edge of a road, and pass the boat-launching area before getting to what looks like a real trail (Jenny Lake Trail).

Follow this trail for less than half a mile to the junction with the Moose Ponds Trail, which is on top of a glacial moraine at the south end of Jenny Lake. Go left (west) on the Moose Ponds Trail and drop down a short but steep slope to the Moose Ponds. The trail winds through willow flats and over footbridges around the three ponds. Watch for elk and moose on the slopes above and waterfowl on the ponds.

After leaving the Moose Ponds, go through a short section of mature forest and then out into the sagebrush flats of Lupine Meadows. The last mile of the hike can be confusing as you cross the unpaved road to the Lupine Meadows Trailhead twice and go behind the Exum Climbing School before getting back to the South Jenny Lake area.

Key Points

0.1 Footbridge over Cottonwood Creek, the outlet to Jenny Lake.

0.3 Boat-launching area; junction with Jenny Lake Trail.

0.6 Junction with Moose Ponds Trail; turn left.

2.0 Lupine Meadows Road.

2.3 Lupine Meadows Road.

2.5 Exum Climbing School.

2.6 South Jenny Lake Visitor Center.

Options: This loop hike can be taken in either direction with no extra difficulty. You can also make this an add-on to the Jenny Lake hike.

Camping: No camping is allowed on this route.

9 String Lake

Short day hikes really don't get much nicer than this one, a flat loop around a gorgeous mountain lake in the shadow of the high peaks. It's also a good choice for an early-season hike because the snow usually leaves the area long before it gives up the high country.

Start: String Lake Trailhead.
Distance: 3.4-mile loop.
Difficulty: Easy.
Seasons: July through September.

Maps: Earthwalk Press Grand Teton map; National Park Service handout map.
Trail contact: Grand Teton National Park, P.O. Drawer 170, Moose, WY 83012; (307) 739-3309; www.nps.gov/grte/.

Finding the trailhead: Take U.S. Highway 89 north of Jackson for 11.5 miles and turn left (west) at the Moose Junction. Drive past the Moose Visitor Center (see Locator Map) and through the entrance station (about a mile after turning off the highway). Follow this paved park road for another 9.7 miles from the entrance station to the Jenny Lake turnoff. Turn left (west) and drive 0.6 mile (follow the signs and take two right turns) to the String Lake Trailhead. From the north, drive 9.9 miles from the Jackson Lake Junction and turn right (west) at the Jenny Lake turnoff. Park in large parking lots at the String Lake Trailhead. There are no toilet facilities at the String Lake Trailhead, but you can find them at the nearby picnic area.

The Hike

On the String Lake Trail, the first 0.3 mile is wheelchair accessible with spectacular views of the Teton Range over placid String Lake. This is a piedmont lake formed by valley glaciers at the head of Paintbrush Canyon. The same goes for Jenny Lake at the head of Cascade Canyon and Leigh Lake at the head of Leigh Canyon.

After passing by the picnic area and parking lot, the trail is no longer wheelchair accessible, but it is still double wide and in terrific shape and offers more sandy beaches and outstanding views.

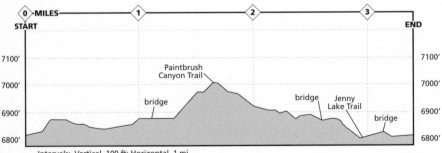

The west side of String Lake.

At the end of the lake, go left (west) at the junction. You immediately reach a long footbridge over the short but scenic stream connecting String Lake and Leigh Lake. From the bridge, walk through a mature forest up to the junction with the Paintbrush Canyon Trail. Go left (south), and walk through mostly open terrain down to the west shoreline of String Lake. The views are not quite as nice here with no Teton Range backdrop, but they are still quite worthwhile. At the next junction, go left (east), cross the unnamed stream between String Lake and Jenny Lake on another big footbridge, and you're back at the trailhead.

Key Points

0.3   String Lake Picnic Area.

0.7   Horse trail comes in from the east.

1.1   End of String Lake and junction with loop trail; turn left.

1.2   Bridge over String Creek.

1.8   Junction with Paintbrush Canyon Trail; turn left.

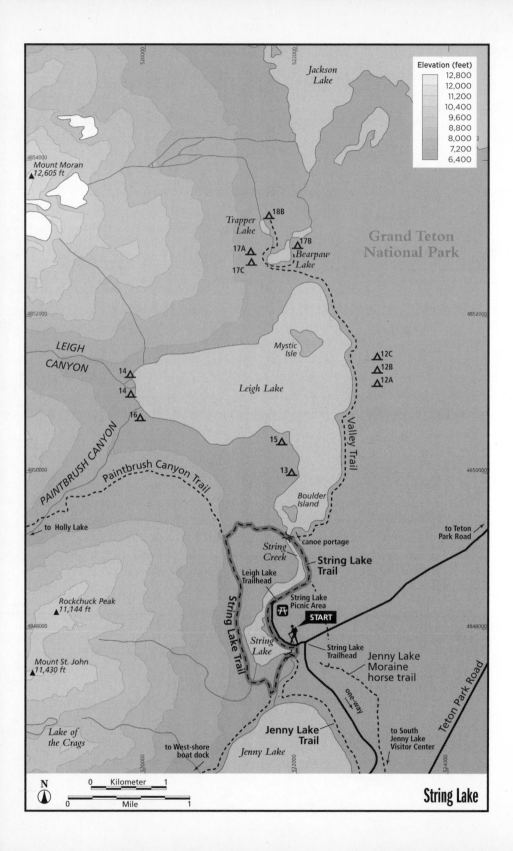

String Lake

3.1 Junction with Jenny Lake Trail; turn left.

3.3 Bridge over String Creek.

3.4 String Lake Trailhead.

Options: This loop hike can be taken in either direction with no extra difficulty.

Side trip: If you need more hiking, hike down to the head of Jenny Lake (0.4-mile round trip) or the foot of Leigh Lake (0.3-mile round trip).

Camping: No camping is allowed on this route.

10 Taggart Lake

The short loop day hike to low-elevation Taggart Lake, named for the chief geologist of the 1872 Hayden Expedition, is one of the most accessible and popular short day hikes in the park. The trail is in great shape all the way, with a few rocky sections.

Start: Taggart Lake Trailhead.
Distance: 4.0-mile loop.
Difficulty: Easy.
Seasons: July through September.
Maps: Earthwalk Press Grand Teton map;
National Park Service trail guide to Taggart and Bradley lakes.
Trail contact: Grand Teton National Park, P.O. Drawer 170, Moose, WY 83012; (307) 739-3309; www.nps.gov/grte/.

Finding the trailhead: Take U.S. Highway 89 north of Jackson for 11.5 miles and turn left (west) at the Moose Junction. Drive past the Moose Visitor Center (see Locator Map) and through the entrance station (about a mile after turning off the highway). Follow this paved park road for another 2.2 miles from the entrance station and turn left (west) to the Taggart Lake Trailhead parking lot. From the north, drive 17.4 miles from the Jackson Lake Junction and turn right (west) into the trailhead parking lot. This trailhead has toilet facilities and plenty of parking.

The Hike

The first 0.3 mile of the trail to the first junction is double wide and flat and goes through a sagebrush-dotted meadow. At the junction, go right (northwest) and the trail becomes singletrack and goes past some minor development and on to Taggart Creek, which you cross on a sturdy footbridge. After the creek, the trail climbs gradually up to the top of a moraine where you get consistently good views of the Teton Range, including Grand Teton. This section of the trail also goes through an old forest-fire burn, so you can observe how the forest is regenerating.

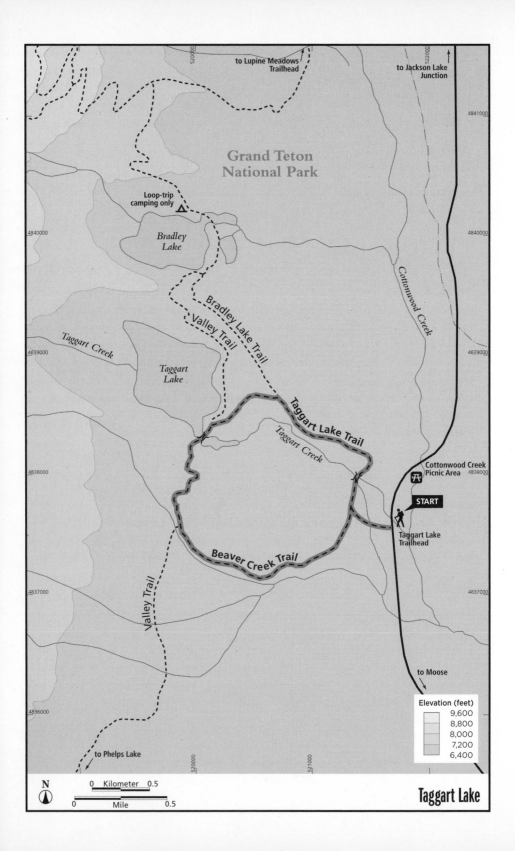

to Lupine Meadows
Trailhead

to Jackson Lake
Junction

Grand Teton
National Park

Loop-trip
camping only

Bradley
Lake

Cottonwood Creek

Taggart Creek

Bradley Lake Trail

Valley Trail

Taggart
Lake

Taggart Lake Trail

Taggart Creek

Cottonwood Creek
Picnic Area

START

Taggart Lake
Trailhead

Beaver Creek Trail

Valley Trail

to Moose

to Phelps Lake

Elevation (feet)

9,600
8,800
8,000
7,200
6,400

N

0   Kilometer   0.5

0   Mile   0.5

Taggart Lake

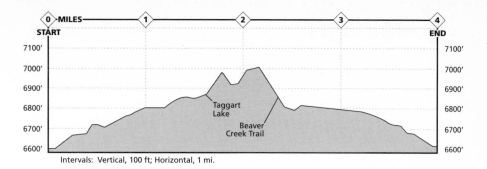

Intervals: Vertical, 100 ft; Horizontal, 1 mi.

When you reach the junction with the Bradley Lake Trail, go left (west) and continue for another 0.6 mile to the lake and the junction with the Valley Trail. Go left (south), and hike along the lakeshore to a large footbridge over the outlet.

Forest-lined Taggart Lake sits at only 6,902 feet at the foot of Avalanche Canyon. You get a gorgeous view of Grand Teton over the lake on the horizon. Look around and see how glaciers left a moraine, which formed a natural dam to create the lake.

After leaving the lake, hike on the Valley Trail for 0.8 mile to the junction with the Beaver Creek Trail. Go left (east) and follow Beaver Creek until you climb over a small hill (bigger if you take the loop counterclockwise) and drop down to the sagebrush flat to the junction with the loop trail and back to the trailhead.

Key Points

- **0.3** Start of loop trail; turn right.
- **0.8** Taggart Creek.
- **1.0** Junction with Bradley Lake Trail; turn left.
- **1.6** Taggart Lake.
- **2.4** Junction with Beaver Creek Trail; turn left.
- **3.8** End of loop; turn right.
- **4.0** Taggart Lake Trailhead.

Options: You can take the loop in either direction with no major increase in difficulty.

Camping: No camping is allowed on this route.

11 Garnet Canyon

Garnet Canyon is a main artery to several popular climbing routes in the park. Expect to see lots of people on the trail and a large parking lot full of vehicles at the trailhead. Still, it's a nice day hike with limited hill climbing.

Start: Lupine Meadows Trailhead.
Distance: 8.2 miles out and back.
Difficulty: Moderate.
Seasons: Mid-July through mid-September.

Maps: Earthwalk Press Grand Teton map; National Park Service handout map.
Trail contact: Grand Teton National Park, P.O. Drawer 170, Moose, WY 83012; (307) 739-3309; www.nps.gov/grte/.

Finding the trailhead: Take U.S. Highway 89 north of Jackson for 11.5 miles and turn left (west) at the Moose Junction. Drive past the Moose Visitor Center (see Locator Map) and through the entrance station (about a mile after turning off the highway). Follow this paved park road for another 6.6 miles from the entrance station and turn left (west) onto a gravel road at the Lupine Meadows turnoff. Follow this road for 1.4 miles until it ends at the trailhead parking lot. From the north, drive 21.8 miles from the Jackson Lake Junction and turn right (west) at the Lupine Meadows turnoff.

The trailhead has toilet facilities and a huge parking area, but this trailhead is so popular that it can be full, especially at midday. You can find a general store at the South Jenny turnoff about a mile to the north.

The Hike

From Lupine Meadows, the first 0.5 mile of the trail goes through mature forest with nice views of Grand Teton to the right. It then climbs up a ridge to the junction with the Garnet Canyon Trail, which also goes to Surprise and Amphitheater lakes. Turn right (west) and start a series of switchbacks up to the junction with the Garnet Canyon Trail. Go left (south) and hike on a gradually ascending trail above the stream to where it ends in a large boulder field. You get a nice view of Middle

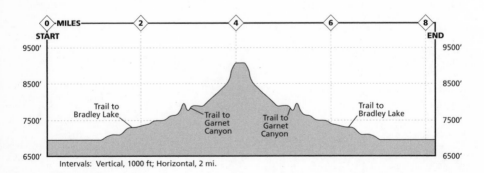

Intervals: Vertical, 1000 ft; Horizontal, 2 mi.

Hiking up Garnet Canyon with Middle Teton in the background.

Teton much of the way up the canyon. You can actually hike farther up the canyon, and many climbers do. In fact, you'll probably see groups of climbers scrambling out through the boulders. From this point on, however, it is off-trail hiking. After a rest, retrace your steps to the Lupine Meadows Trailhead.

Key Points

- **1.7** Junction with trail to Bradley Lake; turn right.
- **3.0** Junction with trail to Garnet Canyon; turn left.
- **4.1** End of maintained trail.

Side trip: You can take the side trip up to Surprise and Amphitheater lakes, which adds 3.6 miles to the total distance of your trip.

Camping: The park service allows camping in the off-trail upper reaches of the canyon. If interested, inquire about camping at the Moose Visitor Center or the Jenny Lake Ranger Station.

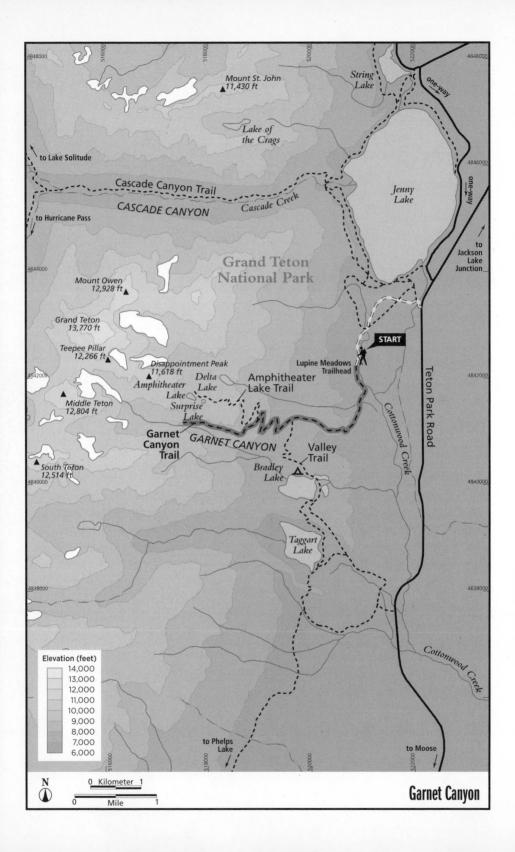

Garnet Canyon

12 Bearpaw and Trapper Lakes

If you like to hike to lakes, this is the best hike in the park. It's very rare to be able to visit four low-elevation lakes (without roads to them!) on one moderate hike without climbing any big hills. This scenic and flat route makes a good day hike or overnighter with a variety of great campsites.

Start: Leigh Lake Trailhead.
Distance: 8.8 miles out and back.
Difficulty: Moderate.
Seasons: July through September.

Maps: Earthwalk Press Grand Teton map; National Park Service handout map
Trail contact: Grand Teton National Park, P.O. Drawer 170, Moose, WY 83012; (307) 739-3309; www.nps.gov/grte/.

Trapper Lake

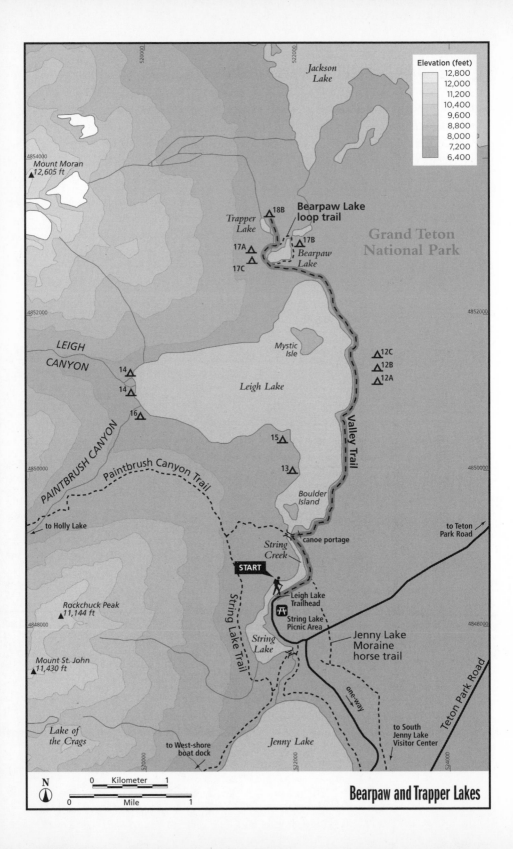

Jackson
Lake

Elevation (feet)

| 12,800 |
| 12,000 |
| 11,200 |
| 10,400 |
| 9,600 |
| 8,800 |
| 8,000 |
| 7,200 |
| 6,400 |

4854000

Mount Moran
▲12,605 ft

520000

522000

**Bearpaw Lake
loop trail**

△18B

Trapper
Lake

△17B

17A △

△ *Bearpaw
Lake*

17C △

**Grand Teton
National Park**

4852000

4852000

LEIGH

*Mystic
Isle*

△12C

△12B

CANYON

14 △

Leigh Lake

△12A

14 △

16 △

Valley Trail

PAINTBRUSH CANYON

15 △

4850000

Paintbrush Canyon Trail

13 △

4850000

to Holly Lake

*Boulder
Island*

to Teton
Park Road

*String
Creek*

canoe portage

START

String Lake Trail

Leigh Lake
Trailhead

Rockchuck Peak
▲11,144 ft

4848000

String Lake
Picnic Area

**Jenny Lake
Moraine
horse trail**

4848000

Mount St. John
▲11,430 ft

*String
Lake*

one-way

Teton Park Road

to South
Jenny Lake
Visitor Center

*Lake of
the Crags*

to West-shore
boat dock

Jenny Lake

520000

522000

524000

N

| 0 | Kilometer | 1 |

| 0 | Mile | 1 |

Bearpaw and Trapper Lakes

Finding the trailhead: Take U.S. Highway 89 north of Jackson for 11.5 miles and turn left (west) at the Moose Junction. Drive past the Moose Visitor Center (see Locator Map) and through the entrance station (about a mile after turning off the highway). Follow this paved park road for another 9.7 miles from the entrance station to the Jenny Lake turnoff. Turn left (west) and drive 0.6 mile (follow the signs and take two right turns) past the String Lake Trailhead and, 0.3 farther, to the String Lake Picnic Area. The Leigh Lake Trailhead is in the northwest corner of the picnic area. From the north, drive 9.9 miles from the Jackson Lake Junction and turn right (west) at the Jenny Lake turnoff. Park in the large parking lot at the picnic area. There are toilet facilities at the Leigh Lake Trailhead.

The Hike

For details on the first part of this route, refer to the String Lake and Leigh Lake hike descriptions.

When you leave Leigh Lake, you pass through a forested area, part of which is recovering nicely from a 1981 forest fire. Just before you reach Bearpaw Lake, you enter a large meadow. The junction for the loop around the lake is in the middle of this meadow. You can obviously take the loop either way around the lake, but this description follows the clockwise route, so bear left (northwest) at this junction.

As you near the lake, the trail drops down into the trees surrounding the shore and follows the shoreline to campsites 17A and 17B. The trails around these two campsites can get confusing, so be alert. The trail to Trapper Lake stays low and goes over a makeshift footbridge over the inlet to Bearpaw Lake and then up on a small ridge where it turns north and heads for Trapper Lake.

After 0.4 mile of walking a level, forest-lined trail, you come to Trapper Lake. There is a nice bench with an overlook of Trapper Lake, a good place for a relaxing lunch to the music of trout jumping in the lake. Campsite 18B is slightly farther up the trail toward the inlet of the lake.

Retrace your steps to Bearpaw Lake. You can go back around the west side of the lake, but you can also take a social trail over to campsite 17B on the northeast shore of the lake where there is an official trail back to the junction south of the lake. The social trail requires a little agility, as you have to cross over the shallow outlet of Bearpaw Lake on logs and rocks.

From the junction, retrace your steps back to the String Lake Picnic Area.

Key Points

0.4 Horse trail comes in from the east.

0.8 End of String Lake and junction with trail to Holly Lake; turn right.

1.0 Leigh Lake.

2.4 East-shore campsites.

2.7 End of Leigh Lake.

Crossing a shallow bay on the north side of Bearpaw Lake to make a loop around the lake.

3.3 Junction with loop trail around Bearpaw Lake.

4.0 North end of Bearpaw Lake.

4.4 Trapper Lake.

Options: If you don't want to retrace your steps all the way, you can turn right (west) at the junction at the end of String Lake and take the String Lake Loop Trail back to the picnic area. This adds 2.5 miles to your hike.

Camping: Refer to the Leigh Lake hike description for details on the Leigh Lake campsites.

Bearpaw Lake has three campsites. Three-star 17A is on the west shore near the lake but has a marginal view of it. It has two tent sites, a fire pit, and good access to water, but the trail goes right by the campsite. Four-star 17C is up the hill from 17A and is more private with a slightly better view. It also has a fire pit and good access to water from the inlet to the lake. These two campsites share the same bear box and bear pole. Five-star 17B is on the northeast shore of the lake by the outlet. It has a terrific view of the lake and the Teton Range in the background, good access to water, a fire pit, a bear box, and is reasonably private.

Trapper Lake has one campsite. Five-star 18B is near the outlet, has a fire pit and a nicerview, and is close to water.

13 Surprise and Amphitheater Lakes

This is a popular hike to two high-country lakes in the shadow of Grand Teton, so expect to see lots of people on the trail and a large parking lot full of vehicles at the trailhead. Day hike or overnighter.

Start: Lupine Meadows Trailhead.
Distance: 9.6 miles out and back.
Difficulty: Moderate.
Seasons: Mid-July through mid-September.

Maps: Earthwalk Press Grand Teton map; National Park Service handout map.
Trail contact: Grand Teton National Park, P.O. Drawer 170, Moose, WY 83012; (307) 739-3309; www.nps.gov/grte/.

Finding the trailhead: Take U.S. Highway 89 north of Jackson for 11.5 miles and turn left (west) at the Moose Junction. Drive past the Moose Visitor Center (see Locator Map) and through the entrance station (about a mile after turning off the highway). Follow this paved park road for another 6.6 miles from the entrance station and turn left (west) onto a gravel road at the Lupine Meadows turnoff. Follow this road for 1.4 miles until it ends at the trailhead parking lot. From the north, drive 21.8 miles from the Jackson Lake Junction and turn right (west) at the Lupine Meadows turnoff.

The trailhead has toilet facilities and a huge parking area, but this trailhead is so popular that it can be full, especially at midday. You can find a general store at the South Jenny turnoff about a mile to the north.

The Hike

From Lupine Meadows, the first 0.5 mile of the Valley Trail goes through mature forest with nice views of Grand Teton off to the right and then climbs up a ridge to the junction with the trail to Garnet Canyon, which also goes to Surprise and Amphitheater lakes. Turn right (west) and start a series of switchbacks up to the lakes. At several points, you get sweeping views of Bradley and Taggart lakes to the southeast and Jenny Lake to the northeast, as well as the rest of the valley floor.

At the 3.0-mile mark; turn right (west) again at the junction with the trail up Garnet Canyon. When you get to Surprise Lake, the only surprise will be how beautiful it is, with Teepee Pillar, Disappointment Peak, Mount Owen, and much more of the Teton Range, including Grand Teton, majestically looming in the background

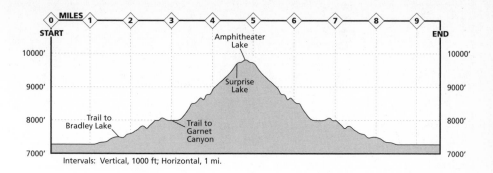

Intervals: Vertical, 1000 ft; Horizontal, 1 mi.

over the lake. Amphitheater Lake, only 0.2 mile up the trail, is at least as nice with an amphitheater view of the high peaks.

After enjoying these two gems of the Teton Range, retrace your steps to the Lupine Meadows Trailhead.

Key Points

1.7   Junction with trail to Bradley Lake; turn right.

3.0   Junction with trail to Garnet Canyon; turn right.

4.6   Surprise Lake.

4.8   Amphitheater Lake.

Side trip: You can take the side trip up to the end of Garnet Canyon, which adds 2.2 miles to the total distance of your trip.

Camping: Surprise Lake has three designated campsites on a ridge on the east side of the lake with a mostly obstructed view of the lake and the high peaks and a moderate walk to water.

 *Amphitheater Lake.*

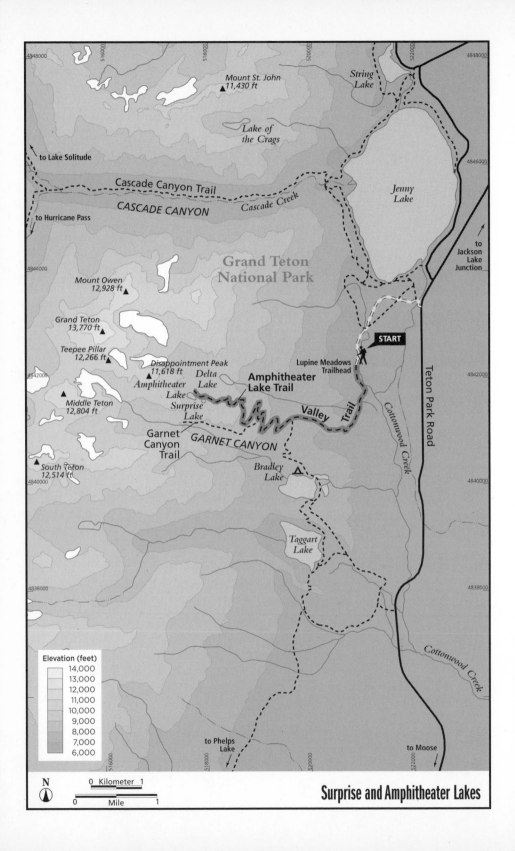

Surprise and Amphitheater Lakes

14 Jenny Lake

Jenny Lake is a great loop hike around one of the centerpieces of Grand Teton National Park. There aren't many hikes of this distance that follow the shoreline of a beautiful lake the entire way. This makes the Jenny Lake loop one of the most popular in Grand Teton National Park.

Start: String Lake Trailhead.
Distance: 7.7-mile loop.
Difficulty: Easy.
Seasons: July through September.

Maps: Earthwalk Press Grand Teton map; National Park Service handout map.
Trail contact: Grand Teton National Park, P.O. Drawer 170, Moose, WY 83012; (307) 739-3309; www.nps.gov/grte/.

Finding the trailhead: Take U.S. Highway 89 north of Jackson for 11.5 miles and turn left (west) at the Moose Junction. Drive past the Moose Visitor Center (see Locator Map) and through the entrance station (about a mile after turning off the highway). Follow this paved park road for another 9.7 miles from the entrance station to the Jenny Lake turnoff. Turn left (west) and drive 0.6 mile (follow the signs and take two right turns) to the String Lake Trailhead and Picnic Area. From the north, drive 9.9 miles from the Jackson Lake Junction and turn right (west) at the Jenny Lake turnoff. If you plan to start at South Jenny Lake, go to the South Jenny Lake turnoff, which is 2.9 miles south of the Jenny Lake turnoff on the main park road.

Park in large parking lots at the trailhead or the picnic area. There are no toilet facilities right at the trailhead, but you can find them at the nearby picnic area. The South Jenny Lake area has a general store, visitor center, boat dock, toilet facilities, and plenty of room to park.

The Hike

You can start at either South Jenny Lake or the String Lake Trailhead at the north end of Jenny Lake. This trail description follows the counterclockwise route starting from the String Lake Trailhead. This allows you to hike the more remote west side of the lake in the morning hours, stop for a snack at the South Jenny Lake general store, visit a visitor center without driving to it, and enjoy a scenic walk along the developed east shore after lunch.

The trail starts about 100 yards south of the trailhead parking lot at the bridge over the huge stream leaving String Lake. Go right (west) and cross the bridge. In 0.2 mile, you turn left (south) at the junction with the String Lake Trail.

After this junction, hike along the unnamed stream between String Lake and Jenny Lake for about two-tenths of a mile to the first view of Jenny Lake at the inlet. The trail then follows the lakeshore until you get near the boat dock area on the west side of the lake. You won't see many hikers on the trail to the boat dock, but expect to see lots of people in the boat dock area, as the boat ride across Jenny Lake is very popular. Many park visitors take the boat over to see Hidden Falls and Inspiration Point.

Hiking the Jenny Lake Trail, one of the most popular in the park.

As you approach the boat dock area, the trail veers away from the lake slightly. You don't see the boat dock unless you take a short spur trail down to the lake. You might not need to do that, but you definitely want to take the 0.8-mile round trip up to see Hidden Falls and to soak in the view from Inspiration Point.

After being inspired from Inspiration Point, continue along the lake to the South Jenny Lake area. The trail closely follows the lakeshore after the boat dock area but gradually pulls away from the lake as you reach the junction with the Moose Ponds Trail. Go left (south) at this junction. The west-side trail gets rocky in a few places but is mostly flat and uncrowded.

The developed south section of Jenny Lake can get confusing, but if you stay on the trail near the lake you eventually come to the visitor center area. You pass by the Jenny Lake boat-launching area, a developed campground, other buildings and developments, and then over a long footbridge over the outlet of Jenny Lake (Cottonwood Creek) and on to the visitor center area. This is slightly more than halfway through the hike, so it's a good time to lay back, get a snack at the general store, and

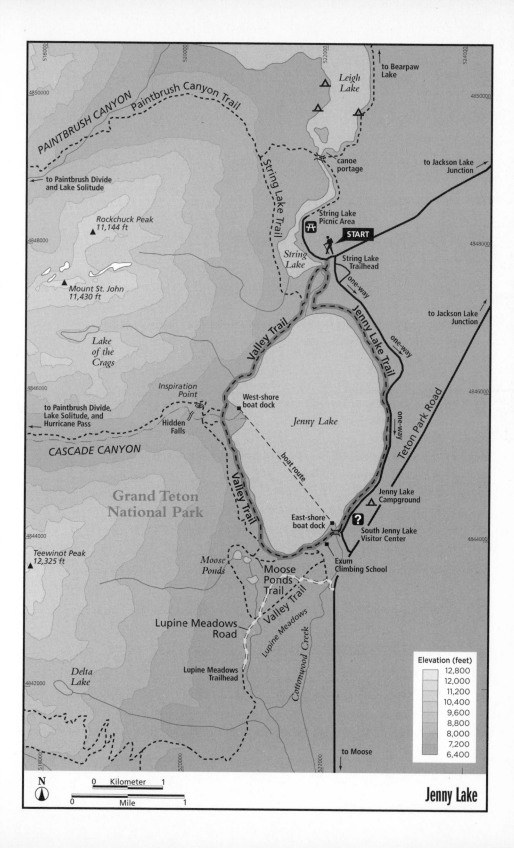

PAINTBRUSH CANYON

Paintbrush Canyon Trail

Leigh Lake

to Bearpaw Lake

canoe portage

to Jackson Lake Junction

to Paintbrush Divide and Lake Solitude

String Lake Trail

String Lake Picnic Area

START

Rockchuck Peak
11,144 ft

String Lake Trailhead

String Lake

one-way

Mount St. John
11,430 ft

one-way

Jenny Lake Trail

to Jackson Lake Junction

Lake of the Crags

Inspiration Point

West-shore boat dock

Jenny Lake

Valley Trail

one-way

Teton Park Road

to Paintbrush Divide, Lake Solitude, and Hurricane Pass

Hidden Falls

boat route

CASCADE CANYON

Grand Teton National Park

Valley Trail

Jenny Lake Campground

East-shore boat dock

South Jenny Lake Visitor Center

?

Teewinot Peak
12,325 ft

Moose Ponds

Moose Ponds

Exum Climbing School

Moose Ponds Trail

Valley Trail

Lupine Meadows Road

Lupine Meadows

Cottonwood Creek

Delta Lake

Lupine Meadows Trailhead

to Moose

Elevation (feet)

12,800
12,000
11,200
10,400
9,600
8,800
8,000
7,200
6,400

N

0   Kilometer   1

0   Mile   1

Jenny Lake

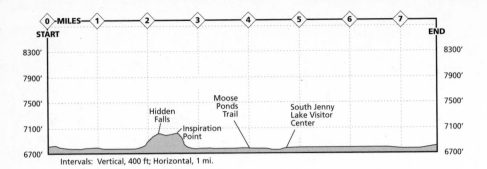

Intervals: Vertical, 400 ft; Horizontal, 1 mi.

check out the interpretive displays in the visitor center before continuing up the east shore of the lake.

The trail through the developed area is paved, but the pavement ends about 0.2 mile up the lakeshore. The east shore is more heavily used than the west shore, and the one-way scenic drive parallels the trail for part of the way. However, the scenery could be considered better than that along the west shore since you get classic views of the high peaks across the lake. The trail is in better shape than on the west side, too.

Key Points

0.1 Bridge over outlet of String Lake.

0.5 Jenny Lake inlet.

2.2 West-shore boat dock and spur trail to Hidden Falls/Inspiration Point.

4.0 Junction with Moose Ponds Trail; turn left.

4.3 Boat-launching area.

4.5 Bridge over Cottonwood Creek, outlet of Jenny Lake.

4.6 South Jenny Lake Boat Dock/Visitor Center; start of paved trail.

4.8 End of paved trail.

7.7 String Lake Trailhead.

Options: This loop hike can be taken in either direction with no extra difficulty. You can also make this a shuttle and skip the developed east side of the lake by leaving a vehicle at one end and hiking only the remote west side of the lake to see Hidden Falls. This cuts the total distance down to 4.8 miles.

Side trip: Don't miss the 0.4-mile (round-trip) side trip to see Hidden Falls, and keep going up to Inspiration Point (another 0.4-mile round trip) for a panoramic view of Jenny Lake.

Camping: No camping is allowed on this route.

15 Holly Lake

Holly Lake is gradual uphill hike to a mountain lake in one of the famous canyons of the Teton Range. Starting at the Leigh Lake Trailhead instead of the String Lake Trailhead gives you great scenery for the first 0.8 mile along the east shore of String Lake. In the morning hours when the skies are more likely to be clear, you can soak in the spectacular views of the Teton Range across String Lake. You can also start at the trailhead and hike the west shore of String Lake in the morning, but I prefer this route. Day hike or overnighter.

Start: Leigh Lake Trailhead.
Distance: 12.7 miles out and back.
Difficulty: Difficult day hike; moderate overnighter.
Seasons: July through September.

Maps: Earthwalk Press Grand Teton map; National Park Service handout map.
Trail contact: Grand Teton National Park, P.O. Drawer 170, Moose, WY 83012; (307) 739-3309; www.nps.gov/grte/.

Finding the trailhead: Take U.S. Highway 89 north of Jackson for 11.5 miles and turn left (west) at the Moose Junction. Drive past the Moose Visitor Center (see Locator Map) and through the entrance station (about a mile after turning off the highway). Follow this paved park road for another 9.7 miles from the entrance station to the Jenny Lake turnoff. Turn left (west) and drive 0.6 mile (follow the signs and take two right turns) to the String Lake Trailhead and, 0.3 mile farther, the String Lake Picnic Area. The Leigh Lake Trailhead is in the northwest corner of the parking lot. From the north, drive 9.9 miles from the Jackson Lake Junction and turn right (west) at the Jenny Lake turnoff. You can also start this hike at the String Lake Trailhead, which is 0.3 mile before the picnic area. Park in the large parking lot at the picnic area. There are toilet facilities right at the Leigh Lake Trailhead.

The Hike

After the first 0.8 mile on a double-wide trail, take a left (west) at the junction at the north end of String Lake. The trail immediately crosses over the inlet of String Lake on a long footbridge and then goes through mature forest until you reach the Paintbrush Canyon Trail 0.8 mile later. Go right (northwest) and start a gradual ascent up Paintbrush Canyon.

As you climb, the forest gradually thins out, and the higher you go the more colorful it gets. This canyon not only has lots of Indian paintbrush but many other species of wildflowers. Take a moment to look behind you for a nice view of Leigh Lake and Jackson Lake.

When you get to the junction with the Holly Lake Trail, go right (north) for a fairly steep 0.5-mile climb to the little jewel of a lake in the shadow of Mount Woodring. I saw a huge black bear on the slope above the lake while having lunch there.

After a good rest at the lake, retrace your steps back to the Paintbrush Canyon Trail and proceed to the junction with the String Lake Trail. From this junction, you can go

Beautiful Holly Lake with Leigh Lake and Jackson Lake in the background.

back the way you came, or you can complete the loop around String Lake. If you choose the loop option; go right (south) and hike about a half mile through mostly open slope down to the west shore of String Lake, where the trail stays most of the rest of the way to the junction with the Jenny Lake Trail. Go left (east) and over the outlet of String Lake 0.2 mile later. At the end of the footbridge; go left (north) and follow the paved trail back to the String Lake Picnic Area and the Leigh Lake Trailhead.

Key Points

- **0.4** Horse trail comes in from the east.
- **0.8** End of String Lake and junction with trail to Holly Lake; turn left.
- **0.9** Footbridge over inlet of String Lake.
- **1.6** Paintbrush Canyon Trail; turn right.
- **5.8** Junction with Holly Lake Trail; turn right.
- **6.3** Holly Lake.

Options: If you want to retrace your steps all the way, go left (east) when you get back to the String Lake Trail, but this only cuts 0.1 mile off your trip.

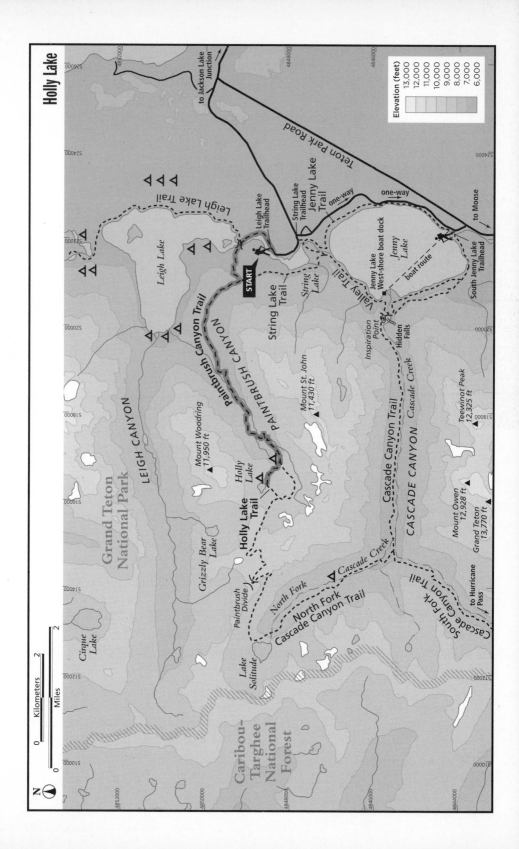

Holly Lake

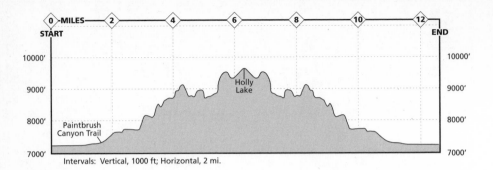

Intervals: Vertical, 1000 ft; Horizontal, 2 mi.

Camping: The lower Paintbrush Canyon Camping Zone has nine indicated campsites strategically located on high points above the trail. Most of them are private (about 100 yards from the trail) but have only one tent pad (the park service plans to add more later). Some of them require a fairly long hike to water. Most are excellent campsites with a good view. This is an experimental camping zone where the park service is assessing the impact of designated campsites compared to the open camping available in most camping zones in the park.

You can also camp at one of three other designated campsites. These campsites are about a quarter mile from the lake at the end of a trail that crosses the outlet on rocks and goes up on a slope above the lake. Campsite 3 is the most private but, surprisingly, the campsites do not have good views right from camp. Water is fairly accessible from all three sites, which have two tent pads each and share a bear box.

16 Cascade Canyon

This is a classic hike into the main canyon below Grand Teton. The mouth of Cascade Canyon around Hidden Falls is perhaps the most heavily used spot in Grand Teton National Park. Thousands of park visitors take the scenic boat ride across Jenny Lake and mill around Hidden Falls and Inspiration Point for a while and then return. The area shows the wear and tear of this heavy use. But there's a reason for the heavy use. The falls are spectacular, and you definitely can get inspired from Inspiration Point. Most visitors to Hidden Falls do not take the scenic hike up Cascade Canyon, so once you've gone past Inspiration Point, the traffic thins out dramatically. Day hike.

Start: Jenny Lake West-shore boat dock.
Distance: Up to 9.8 miles out and back.
Difficulty: Moderate.
Seasons: July through September.

Maps: Earthwalk Press Grand Teton map; National Park Service handout map.
Trail contact: Grand Teton National Park, P.O. Drawer 170, Moose, WY 83012; (307) 739-3309; www.nps.gov/grte/.

Cascade Canyon from the east shore of Jenny Lake.

Finding the trailhead: Take U.S. Highway 89 north of Jackson for 11.5 miles and turn left (west) at the Moose Junction. Drive past the Moose Visitor Center (see Locator Map) and through the entrance station (about a mile after turning off the highway). Follow this paved park road for another 6.8 miles from the entrance station to the South Jenny Lake turnoff. Turn left (west) and drive less than 0.5 mile to the South Jenny Lake boat dock and visitor center. From the north, drive 12.8 miles from the Jackson Lake Junction and turn right (west) at the South Jenny Lake turnoff. From the South Jenny Lake Boat Dock, take the short boat ride across the lake to the west-shore boat dock. The boat leaves every fifteen to twenty minutes and requires a small fee.

The South Jenny Lake area has a general store, visitor center, boat dock, toilet facilities, and usually plenty of room to park. This is a heavily used area, and the boat ride across the lake is very popular, so in midday during the summer the parking lot can be full. There are no facilities at the west-shore boat dock.

The Hike

The hike up the canyon climbs seriously for about the first mile and then goes into a gradual, almost unnoticeable ascent along the cascading stream on the Cascade Canyon Trail. The steep canyon gives you one outstanding view after another all the

Hiking up Cascade Canyon.

way to the junction where the trail splits into the South Fork to Hurricane Pass and the North Fork to Lake Solitude and Paintbrush Divide.

After a short rest, turn around and retrace your steps back to Jenny Lake in time to catch the boat back across the lake. If for some reason you miss the boat, you can hike along the south shore of the lake 2.1 miles to the east-shore boat dock.

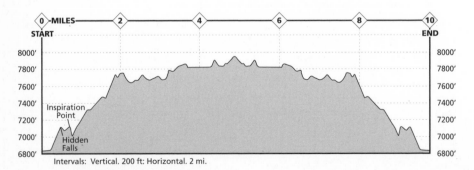

Intervals: Vertical. 200 ft: Horizontal. 2 mi.

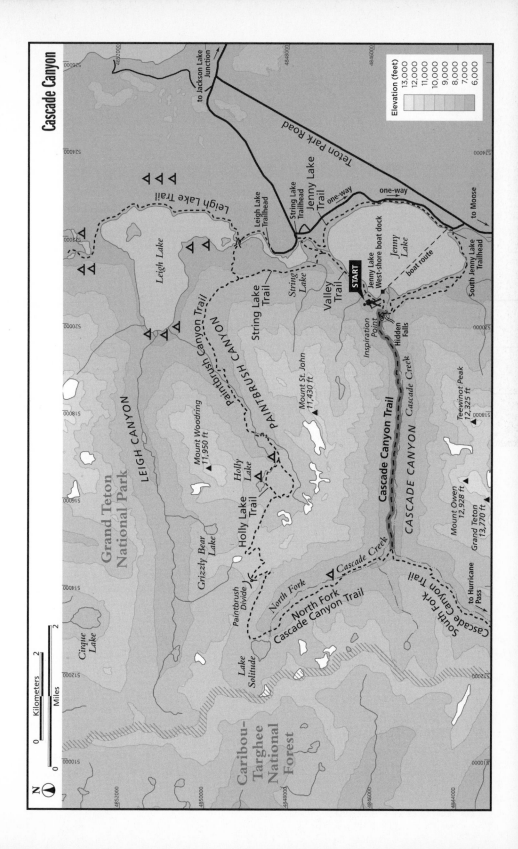

Cascade Canyon

Key Points

0.2 Junction with Valley Trail; go straight onto Cascade Canyon Trail.

0.5 Hidden Falls and junction with spur trail to Hidden Falls Overlook.

0.9 Inspiration Point.

1.6 Horse bypass trail.

4.9 Trail forks into South and North Fork Cascade Canyon Trails.

Options: If you want to leave early in the morning or don't like boats, you can hike along the south shore of Jenny Lake to get to the Hidden Falls area. This would add about 4 miles to your hike.

Camping: No camping is allowed on this route.

17 Lake Solitude

This is a popular hike to the most famous lake that you can't drive to in the Teton Range. Day hike or overnighter.

Start: South Jenny Lake Visitor Center.
Distance: 15.2 miles out and back.
Difficulty: Difficult.
Seasons: Mid-July through mid-September.

Maps: Earthwalk Press Grand Teton map; National Park Service handout map.
Trail contact: Grand Teton National Park, P.O. Drawer 170, Moose, WY 83012; (307) 739-3309; www.nps.gov/grte/.

Finding the trailhead: Take U.S. Highway 89 north of Jackson for 11.5 miles and turn left (west) at the Moose Junction. Drive past the Moose Visitor Center (see Locator Map) and through the entrance station (about one mile after turning off the highway). Follow this paved park road for another 6.8 miles from the entrance station to the South Jenny Lake turnoff. Turn left (west) and drive less than 0.5 mile to the South Jenny Lake Boat Dock and Visitor Center.

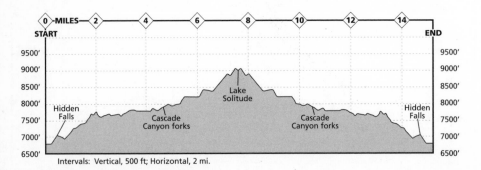

Intervals: Vertical, 500 ft; Horizontal, 2 mi.

Hikers always yield to moose, like this one who wanted the trail while coming down from Lake Solitude. He got what he wanted.

From the north, drive 12.8 miles from the Jackson Lake Junction and turn right (west) at the South Jenny Lake turnoff. From the South Jenny Lake Boat Dock, take the short boat ride across the lake to the west-shore boat dock. The boat leaves every fifteen to twenty minutes and requires a small fee.

The South Jenny Lake area has a general store, visitor center, boat dock, toilet facilities, and usually plenty of room to park. This is a heavily used area, and the boat ride across the lake is very popular, so in midday during the summer the parking lot can be full. There are no facilities at the west-shore boat dock.

The Hike

The mouth of Cascade Canyon around Hidden Falls is perhaps the most heavily used spot in Grand Teton National Park. Thousands of park visitors take the scenic boat ride across Jenny Lake and mill around the falls and Inspiration Point for a while and then return. The area shows the wear and tear of this heavy use. But there's a reason for the heavy use. The falls are spectacular, and you can get inspired from Inspiration Point.

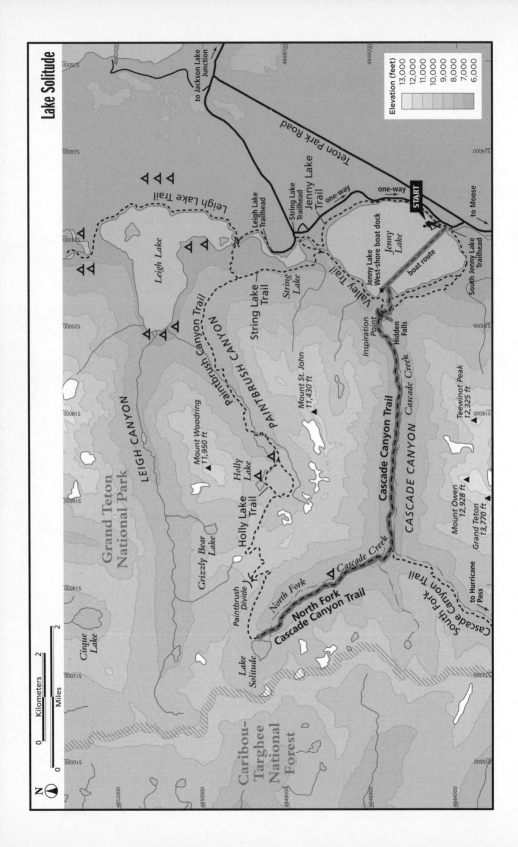

Lake Solitude

Elevation (feet)
13,000
12,000
11,000
10,000
9,000
8,000
7,000
6,000

Grand Teton National Park

Caribou–Targhee National Forest

to Jackson Lake Junction

Teton Park Road

Leigh Lake Trail

Leigh Lake

String Lake Trailhead

Jenny Lake Trail

Leigh Lake Trailhead

one-way

one-way

START

to Moose

Jenny Lake West-shore boat dock

Jenny Lake

boat route

South Jenny Lake Trailhead

Valley Trail

String Lake

String Lake Trail

Inspiration Point

Hidden Falls

Cascade Creek

LEIGH CANYON

Paintbrush Canyon Trail

PAINTBRUSH CANYON

Mount St. John 11,430 ft

Mount Woodring 11,950 ft

Holly Lake

Holly Lake Trail

Grizzly Bear Lake

Cascade Canyon Trail

CASCADE CANYON

Cascade Creek

Teewinot Peak 12,325 ft

Mount Owen 12,928 ft

Grand Teton 13,770 ft

North Fork

Cascade Creek

Paintbrush Divide

North Fork Cascade Canyon Trail

Cascade Creek

South Fork Cascade Canyon Trail

to Hurricane Pass

Lake Solitude

Cirque Lake

N

Kilometers
0   2

Miles
0   2

Most visitors to Hidden Falls do not take the scenic hike up Cascade Canyon, so once you've gone past Inspiration Point, the traffic thins out dramatically.

The hike up the canyon climbs seriously for about the first mile and then goes into a gradual, almost unnoticeable ascent along the cascading stream. The steep canyon gives you one outstanding view after another all the way to the junction where the trail splits into the South Fork up to Hurricane Pass and the North Fork to Lake Solitude and Paintbrush Divide.

Go right (northwest), and start the gradual 2.7-mile upgrade to 9,035-foot Lake Solitude. About halfway up, after crossing the North Fork of Cascade Creek twice on footbridges, you break out of the forest into a wildflower-carpeted cirque, which will be implanted in your memory as one of the most beautiful places you have ever been. The lake itself is at timberline, so only a few scattered trees surround it.

Hiking down the south side of the Paintbrush Divide to Lake Solitude, seen in the distance.

Spend as much time as you have at Lake Solitude and then start the descent to the boat dock. For most of the 2.7 miles down to the main trail, you are staring at Grand Teton along with Mount Owen, Teewinot Peak, and other famous highpoints in the Teton Range. When you reach the main trail, go left (east) and retrace your steps to Jenny Lake. Be sure to start back in time to catch the boat across the lake. If for some reason you miss the boat, you can hike along the south shore of the lake 2.1 miles to the east-shore boat dock.

Key Points

0.2 Junction with Jenny Lake Trail; go straight onto Cascade Canyon Trail.

0.5 Hidden Falls and junction with spur trail to Hidden Falls Overlook.

0.9 Inspiration Point.

1.6 Horse bypass trail.

4.9 Trail splits into South and North Fork Cascade Canyon Trails; turn right.

7.6 Lake Solitude.

Options: If you want to leave early in the morning or don't like boats, you can hike along the south shore of Jenny Lake to get to the Hidden Falls area. This would add about 4 miles to your hike.

Side trip: If you have the energy and time (and make sure you have both), you can extend your trip to the top of Paintbrush Divide, another 2.4 miles above Lake Solitude. This adds 4.8 miles to the total distance of this trip.

Camping: You can camp in the North Fork Cascade Camping Zone, which starts shortly after you turn right at the fork in the main trail and goes up to within about a half mile of the lake. With one or two exceptions, these are memorable campsites with great views in the shadow of Grand Teton. You'll have good access to water, privacy, and two or more tent sites. Even the exceptions are excellent. Keep in mind that you can camp at any of the eleven indicated sites but aren't required to do so. You can set up a no-trace camp anywhere in the camping zone.

18 Valley Trail

This isn't one of the high-country adventures that most people visualize when they think of Grand Teton National Park. Instead, this is a walk in the woods similar to what you would find in many western mountain ranges. The Valley Trail, which goes to three low-elevation lakes, is a popular choice for early spring because the snow gives up this low-elevation area long before the high passes.

The trail is in good shape the entire way with a hill between each lake and canyon. Some sections of the trail, mainly at the south end near Teton Village, receive heavy horse use. The trail goes through a forest mixed with lodgepole, Engelmann spruce, Douglas fir, and aspen. The southern end of the trail has more aspen and turns a wonderful aspen gold in the fall.

Start: Lupine Meadows Trailhead.	**Maps:** Earthwalk Press Grand Teton map;
Distance: 14.9-mile shuttle (day hike or	National Park Service handout map, plus park
overnighter).	service trail guide to Taggart and Bradley
Difficulty: Difficult day hike; moderate	Lakes.
overnighter.	**Trail contact:** Grand Teton National Park, P.O.
Seasons: July through September.	Drawer 170, Moose, WY 83012; (307)
	739-3309; www.nps.gov/grte/.

Finding the trailhead: Take U.S. Highway 89 north of Jackson for 11.5 miles and turn left (west) at the Moose Junction. Drive past the Moose Visitor Center (see Locator Map) and through the entrance station (about a mile after turning off the highway). Follow this paved park road for another 6.6 miles past the entrance station and turn left (west) onto a gravel road at the Lupine Meadows turnoff. Follow this road for 1.4 miles until it ends at the trailhead parking lot. From the north, drive 21.8 miles from the Jackson Lake Junction and turn right (west) at the Lupine Meadows turnoff.

Leave a vehicle or arrange to be picked up at Teton Village, which is 12.5 miles northwest of Jackson. From Jackson, take Highway 22 west of Jackson for about 6 miles to the Moose-Wilson Road junction just before the small town of Wilson. Turn right (north); go 6.5 miles, and turn left (west) into Teton Village.

The trailhead has toilet facilities and a huge parking area, but this trailhead is so popular that it can be full, especially at midday. You can find a general store at the South Jenny Lake turnoff about a mile to the north.

The Hike

From Lupine Meadows, Valley Trail starts out flat through mature forest with nice views of Grand Teton off to the right. Then it climbs up a ridge to the junction with

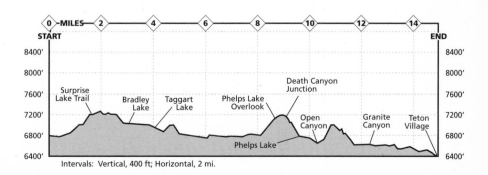

A moose visits camp at Phelps Lake.

the Surprise Lake Trail, which also goes to Garnet Canyon. Turn left (south) and drop down to Bradley Lake. After you have hiked most of the way around the small lake, you see the Bradley Lake Trail veering off to the left. Go right (south) and hike over another ridge (actually a moraine) between Bradley and Taggart lakes. Go right (south) at the junction with the Taggart Lake Trail and do the same 0.8 mile up the trail at the Beaver Creek Trail junction. Both of these trails go off to the east to the Taggart Lake Trailhead.

From Beaver Creek, it's 2.9 miles to the junction to the Death Canyon Trailhead. You can't actually see the trailhead when you get to the junction, but it's only 0.1 mile to the left (east), in case you're looking for a pit toilet. Continue south by going right at this junction as it climbs gradually to a great overlook above Phelps Lake, a fabulous place for a little R&R. It's another 1.1 miles down to Phelps Lake (take a left at the Death Canyon Trail Junction) and, if you're backpacking, your overnight campsite.

The trail skirts the west side of Phelps Lake (watch for moose; they're every-where around Phelps Lake) and then keeps going south through the same terrain. Go left (south) at both junctions with the Open Canyon Trail about a mile after the lake.

When you get to Granite Creek, you see the junction with the trail up Granite Canyon on the north bank of the stream. Go left (south) and cross the sturdy foot-bridge. Just on the other side of the stream is the junction with the trail to the Gran-ite Lake Trailhead, 1.6 miles to the left (east). Go right (south) and head for Teton Village. From here to the park boundary, expect to see large horse parties. Parts of this trail are heavily trampled and resemble long thin feedlots.

After a 1.7-mile hike through aspens and small meadows, you reach the park boundary where the horse use abruptly ends. From this point on, you go through the Teton Village Ski Area to the main lodge. The trail through the ski area can get very confusing. Follow the signs that say SUMMER HIKING TRAIL or VALLEY TRAIL, some of which are on maintenance roads, to the main ski lodge. You can frequently see the main lodge and tram to help stay on the right track.

Key Points

1.7 Junction with Surprise Lake Trail; turn left.

3.1 Bradley Lake.

3.3 Junction with Bradley Lake Trail; turn right.

4.1 Taggart Lake.

4.2 Junction with Taggart Lake Trail; turn right.

5.0 Junction with Beaver Creek Trail; turn right.

7.9 Death Canyon Trailhead; turn right.

8.7 Phelps Lake Overlook.

9.5 Junction with Death Canyon Trail; turn left.

9.8 Phelps Lake.

10.4 First junction with Open Canyon Trail; turn left.

10.6 Second junction with Open Canyon Trail; turn left.

12.3 Junction with Granite Canyon Trail; turn left.

12.4 Junction with trail to Granite Trailhead; turn right.

14.2 Park boundary.

14.9 Teton Village.

Options: You can shorten this shuttle by leaving a vehicle at the Taggart Lake, Death Canyon, or Granite Trailheads.

You can take this shuttle in reverse, of course, which means you face the fairly steep climb up through the ski area. When we hiked this route, we started at Teton Village and had a frustrating experience trying to find the trail amid all the con-

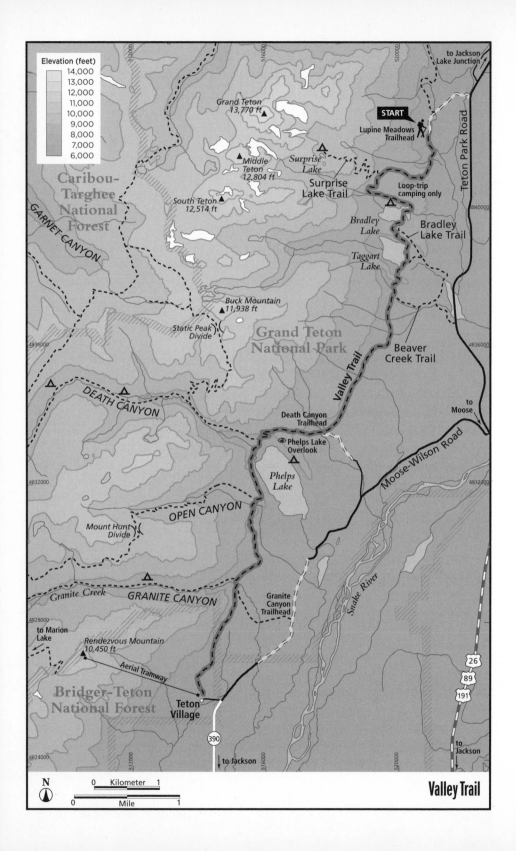

Valley Trail

struction and roads in the first mile. Hiking from the north it should be easier to navigate through the ski area because you can look ahead and see the main ski lodge and tram where the trail ends.

Bailout: The trail goes by five spur trails back to trailheads along the eastern slope of the Teton Range, so you can cut this hike short and bail out along the way.

Camping: Phelps Lake has three five-star designated campsites. As you approach the lake, watch for a junction with a trail going to the left (north) to the campsites. All are on the north shore of the lake with a terrific view of the lake, fire pits, room for two tents, and a shared bear box. The campsites are out of sight of the main trail, but the three campsites are fairly close, so please talk softly to respect the privacy of others.

Bradley Lake also has a designated campsite, but this is reserved for backpackers doing the Grand Teton Loop.

19 Paintbrush Divide

Paintbrush Divide is one of the premier hikes in Grand Teton National Park. It's best to wait until August to try this hike. Snow clings to the north face of Paintbrush Divide until late in the summer, and even in September you can plan on crossing a few snowbanks. If you decide to go earlier, before you leave, check on snow conditions with rangers at the visitor center. This is a long day hike, overnighter, or two-night backpacking trip.

Start: Leigh Lake Trailhead.
Distance: 19.3-mile loop.
Difficulty: Difficult.
Seasons: August and early September.

Maps: Earthwalk Press Grand Teton map; National Park Service handout map
Trail contact: Grand Teton National Park, P.O. Drawer 170, Moose, WY 83012; (307) 739-3309; www.nps.gov/grte/.

Finding the trailhead: Take U.S. Highway 89 north of Jackson for 11.5 miles and turn left (west) at the Moose Junction. Drive past the Moose Visitor Center (see Locator Map) and through the entrance station (about a mile after turning off the highway). Follow this paved park road for another 9.7 miles from the entrance station to the Jenny Lake turnoff. Turn left (west) and drive 0.6 mile (follow the signs and take two right turns) to the String Lake Trailhead and, 0.3 mile farther, the String Lake Picnic Area. The Leigh Lake Trailhead is in the northwest corner of the picnic area. From the north, drive 9.9 miles from the Jackson Lake Junction and turn right (west) at the Jenny Lake turnoff. You can also start this hike at the String Lake Trailhead, which is 0.3 mile before the picnic area. Park in the large parking lot at the picnic area. There are toilet facilities in the picnic area at the Leigh Lake Trailhead.

Even in September, hikers have to cross several snowbanks on the way up the north side of Paintbrush Divide.

The Hike

Starting this hike at the Leigh Lake Trailhead at the picnic area instead of the String Lake Trailhead gives you great scenery for the first 0.8 mile along the east shore of String Lake. You can soak in the spectacular views of the Teton Range across String Lake in the morning hours when the skies are more likely to be clear. You can also start at the String Lake Trailhead and hike the west shore of String Lake in the morning, but I prefer the east-shore route.

After the first 0.8 mile on double-wide trail, take a left (west) at the junction at the north end of String Lake. The trail immediately crosses over the inlet of String Lake on a long footbridge and then goes through mature forest until you reach the Paintbrush Canyon Trail 0.7 mile later. Go right (west) and start a gradual ascent up Paintbrush Canyon.

As you climb the forest gradually thins out, and the higher you go the more colorful it gets. This canyon not only has lots of Indian paintbrush but also many other species of wildflowers. Take a moment to look behind you for a nice view of Leigh Lake and Jackson Lake.

When you get to the junction with the Holly Lake Trail, go right (north) for a fairly steep 0.5-mile climb to the little jewel of a lake in the shadow of Mount Woodring. I saw a huge black bear on the slope above the lake while having lunch there.

After a good rest at the lake, continue for 0.3 mile and rejoin the main Paintbrush Canyon Trail. This means you skip 0.9 mile of trail with your foray over to see Holly Lake, a steeper but shorter route up Paintbrush Canyon.

From here, it's a 1.3-mile climb up above timberline to 10,700-foot Paintbrush Divide. The divide faces north, so plan on crossing a few snowbanks. I hiked up the divide on September 14 and still had to cross four snowbanks. The trail is well contoured to make it seem like a fairly easy ascent.

After enjoying the spectacular scenery from the divide, take an equally scenic route down to Lake Solitude. Most of the way you can see Lake Solitude and Mica Lake and Grand Teton off to the southeast. It doesn't get much better than this.

Lake Solitude is now one of the most popular destinations in the park, so expect to see other hikers. At 9,035 feet, the large lake sits close to timberline and is a fragile environment, so be careful not to leave your mark on what you could call Lake Not-so-Solitude or Lake Multitude.

The scenery remains spectacular after the lake as you head down the North Fork of Cascade Creek. Grand Teton is constantly in your face. If you did this hike clockwise, you'd miss this postcard view. When you reach the junction with the South Fork Trail; go left (east) and head down Cascade Canyon to the boat dock. You cross the creek twice on sturdy footbridges.

Just before you get to Jenny Lake, take a few minutes at Inspiration Point, a beautiful overlook with a sweeping view of Jenny Lake. Less than a half mile later, you pass by huge Hidden Falls, a major waterfall, especially in the spring. There is also a short spur trail off to the right for a great view of Hidden Falls.

About one-tenth of a mile after the falls, you reach a trail leading to the boat dock. Go left here, cross a footbridge, and then take another left onto the Jenny Lake Trail, the main trail around the lake. You don't need to go all the way down to the west-shore boat dock.

The trail follows the shoreline of Jenny Lake for 1.1 miles to the junction with the Paintbrush Canyon Trail. Go right (east), and hike another 0.3 mile to the String Lake Trailhead. From the trailhead, hike a paved trail for 0.3 mile along String Lake to the Leigh Lake Trailhead and the picnic area.

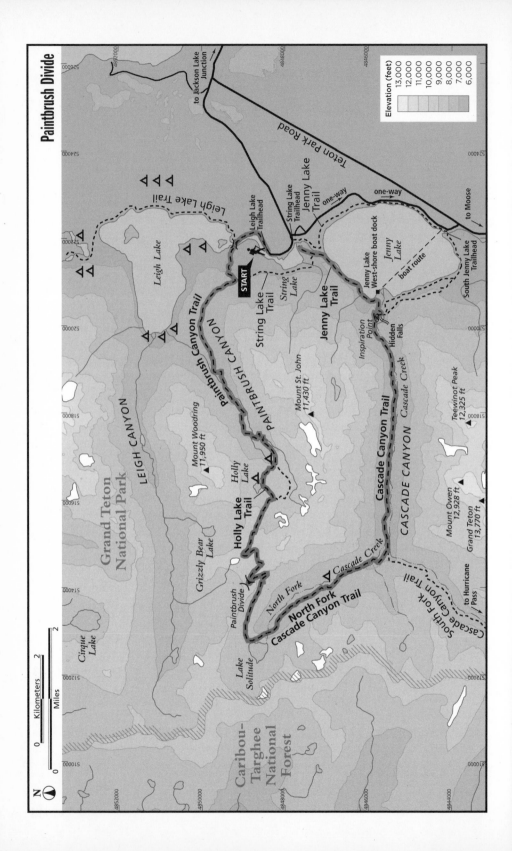

Paintbrush Divide

Elevation (feet)
13,000
12,000
11,000
10,000
9,000
8,000
7,000
6,000

N

Grand Teton National Park

Caribou-Targhee National Forest

LEIGH CANYON

Leigh Lake

Leigh Lake Trail

Paintbrush Canyon Trail

PAINTBRUSH CANYON

String Lake Trail

START

String Lake

Leigh Lake Trailhead

String Lake Trailhead

Jenny Lake Trail

one-way

one-way

Teton Park Road

to Jackson Lake Junction

to Moose

Jenny Lake Trail

Jenny Lake West-shore boat dock

Jenny Lake

boat route

South Jenny Lake Trailhead

Inspiration Point

Hidden Falls

Cascade Canyon Trail

Cascade Creek

CASCADE CANYON

Cascade Creek

Mount St. John 11,430 ft

Mount Woodring 11,950 ft

Holly Lake

Holly Lake Trail

Grizzly Bear Lake

Cirque Lake

Lake Solitude

North Fork

Paintbrush Divide

North Fork Cascade Canyon Trail

Cascade Creek

South Fork Cascade Canyon Trail

to Hurricane Pass

Teewinot Peak 12,325 ft

Mount Owen 12,928 ft

Grand Teton 13,770 ft

Kilometers
Miles

Key Points

0.4   Horse trail comes in from the east.

0.8   End of String Lake; turn left.

0.9   Footbridge over String Creek.

1.6   Paintbrush Canyon Trail; turn right.

5.8   Junction with Holly Lake Trail; turn right.

6.3   Holly Lake.

6.7   Return to Paintbrush Canyon Trail; turn right.

8.0   Paintbrush Divide.

10.4   Lake Solitude; junction with North Fork Cascade Canyon Trail.

13.1   Junction with Cascade Canyon Trail; turn left.

16.4   Horse bypass trail.

17.1   Inspiration Point.

17.5   Hidden Falls.

17.6   Jenny Lake West-shore boat dock and junction with Jenny Lake Trail; turn left.

18.7   Junction with Paintbrush Canyon Trail; turn right.

19.0   String Lake Trailhead.

19.3   String Lake Parking Area/Leigh Lake Trailhead.

Options: You can do this loop hike in reverse, but the climb up to the divide seems easier going on the counterclockwise route described. You can also start and finish the hike at the String Lake Trailhead or at the west-shore boat dock on Jenny Lake after taking the boat across the lake. If you've already seen Inspiration Point and Hidden Falls and are in a hurry, you can take the horse bypass trail to the Jenny Lake Trail and miss this congested area, which cuts about a mile off your trip.

Side trip: If you have enough time and energy, the trail up the South Fork of Cascade Creek to Hurricane Pass would be a memorable trip, but it would add 10.2 miles to the total distance of your trip.

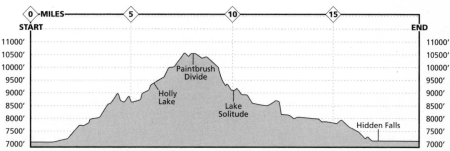

Intervals: Vertical, 500 ft; Horizontal, 5 mi.

Almost to Paintbrush Divide from the north side.

Camping: The lower Paintbrush Canyon Camping Zone has nine indicated camp-sites strategically located on high points above the trail. Most of them are private (about 100 yards from the trail) but have only one tent pad (the park service plans to add more later). Some of them have a fairly long hike to water. Most of the camp-sites are outstanding with a good view.

Holly Lake has three designated campsites. These campsites are about a quarter mile from the lake at the end of a trail that crosses the outlet on rocks and goes up on a slope above the lake. Campsite 3 is the most private, but surprisingly the camp-sites do not have a good view right from camp. Water is fairly accessible from all three sites, which have two tent pads each and share a bear box.

You can also camp along the main trail in the Upper Paintbrush Canyon Camp-ing Zone about a half mile below the lake. This is a different camping zone from Holly Lake, so make sure your permit matches your campsite.

The park service once allowed camping at Lake Solitude, but the campsites were removed because of the heavy use in the area. You can camp just below the lake in the eleven indicated campsites in the North Fork Cascade Camping Zone. Most are five-star or four-star campsites with awesome views of Grand Teton towering over the camp and easy access to water. All campsites are well off the trail with space for at least two tents. Even though the indicated campsites are terrific, you don't have to camp there. You can set up a no-trace camp anywhere else in the North Fork Camping Zone.

20 The Grand Teton Loop

This hike, along with the Teton Crest, offers up the real stuff. It's difficult to really capture the true essence of the Teton Range in a day hike, but with a night or two in the shadows of the high peaks, it creeps into your insides and takes root.

You need at least four days to hike the entire loop and have the time for relaxing for side trips. Even taking this long it's still a tough trip. Because of the position of the camping zones, you are looking at 10-mile-plus days on the last two days. There is no camping zone between Alaska Basin and Phelps Lake (11 miles) or between Phelps Lake and the Lupine Meadows Trailhead (10 miles). This hike description describes a four-day trip, but check the options section below for ways to shorten or lengthen the trip.

The trip starts with a pleasant boat ride across Jenny Lake. You can clearly see the beginning of your route, the mouth of Cascade Canyon, during the fifteen-minute ride.

Start: Jenny Lake West-shore boat dock.
Distance: 32.6-mile loop.
Difficulty: Difficult.
Seasons: Late July through mid-September.
Maps: Earthwalk Press Grand Teton map;

National Park Service handout map.
Trail contact: Grand Teton National Park, P.O. Drawer 170, Moose, WY 83012; (307) 739-3309; www.nps.gov/grte/.
Finding the trailhead: Take U.S. Highway

89 north of Jackson for 11.5 miles and turn left (west) at the Moose Junction. Drive past the Moose Visitor Center (see Locator Map) and through the entrance station (about a mile after turning off the highway). Follow this paved park road for another 6.8 miles from the entrance station to the South Jenny Lake turnoff. Turn left (west) and drive less than 0.5 mile to the South Jenny Lake Boat Dock and Visitor Center. From the north, drive 12.8 miles from the Jackson Lake Junction and turn right (west) at the South Jenny Lake turnoff. From the South Jenny Lake Boat Dock, take the short boat ride across the lake to the west-shore boat dock. The boat leaves every fifteen to twenty minutes for a small fee. If you have two vehicles, you can leave one of them at the Lupine Meadows Trailhead (about a mile walk to the south). The turnoff to Lupine Meadows is about a quarter mile south of the South Jenny turnoff on the main park road.

The South Jenny Lake area has a general store, visitor center, boat dock, toilet facilities, and usually plenty of room to park. This is a heavily used area, and the boat ride across the lake is very popular, so in midday during the summer the parking lot can be full. There are no

Hiking along Static Peak Divide.

facilities at the west-shore boat dock. Lupine Meadows Trailhead also has toilet facilities and plenty of room to park but can also fill up in midday.

The Hike

The mouth of Cascade Canyon around Hidden Falls is perhaps the most heavily used spot in Grand Teton National Park. Thousands of park visitors take the scenic boat ride across Jenny Lake and mill around the falls and Inspiration Point for a while and then return. The area shows the wear and tear of this heavy use. But there's a reason for the heavy use. The falls are spectacular, and you can get really inspired from Inspiration Point.

Most visitors to Hidden Falls do not take the scenic hike up Cascade Canyon, so once you've gone past Inspiration Point, the traffic thins out dramatically. The hike up the canyon climbs seriously for about the first mile and then goes into a gradual, almost unnoticeable ascent along the, of course, cascading stream. However, Cascade Creek also pauses in some smooth-water sections to give a quiet contrast to the steep canyon walls on each side. Mount Owen and Teewinot Peak dominate the southern horizon. The steep canyon gives you one outstanding view after another all the way to the junction where the trail splits into the South Fork up to Hurricane Pass and the North Fork to Lake Solitude and Paintbrush Divide.

Go left (southwest). The grade becomes slightly more precipitous as you head toward Hurricane Pass. Look for a campsite in the early part of the camping zone, which starts shortly after the junction.

The next morning start early enough to have time for a side trip up Avalanche Divide. When you get to the junction with Avalanche Divide, hang your packs and take two or three hours enjoying a truly fantastic view of Grand Teton, Middle Teton, and South Teton, the best view of all three I found anywhere in the park. The trail to the divide is steep and gets a little hard to follow near the divide, but the incredible vistas make the pain and exhaustion go away.

Once back at the junction, start the climb up to Hurricane Pass—a gap in The Wall, a steep cliff along the park boundary. It's a respectable but not brutal climb to

Watch your step on the way to Static Peak Divide.

Schoolroom Glacier viewed from Hurricane Pass.

the pass. The trail is in great shape and nicely switchbacked. At this point it may give you some comfort to know that doing this hike in reverse would be even more difficult, with over 10 miles of steep upgrade in Death Canyon and up to Static Peak Divide.

On top, true to its namesake, it may get a bit breezy (around a category-three hurricane when I was there), but hang onto something long enough to get a memorable view of everything. In addition to the incredible mountain scenery, you can see Schoolroom Glacier right below the pass.

From the pass, it's a short walk on the ridge before dropping down into Alaska Basin. You could call this the "no wimp zone." Anything up here is hardy—the alpine sunflowers, the little willows that might be 100 years old, the overstuffed marmots running around, and, of course, even the mighty backpackers who make it to Alaska Basin.

Once over the ridge and into the basin, you get a sweeping view of the entire basin and Battleship Mountain to the west. The trail goes along the west shore of Sunset Lake and, shortly thereafter, the first of many junctions. To stay on this route, go left (east), but you may want to go over to the Basin Lakes area for your second

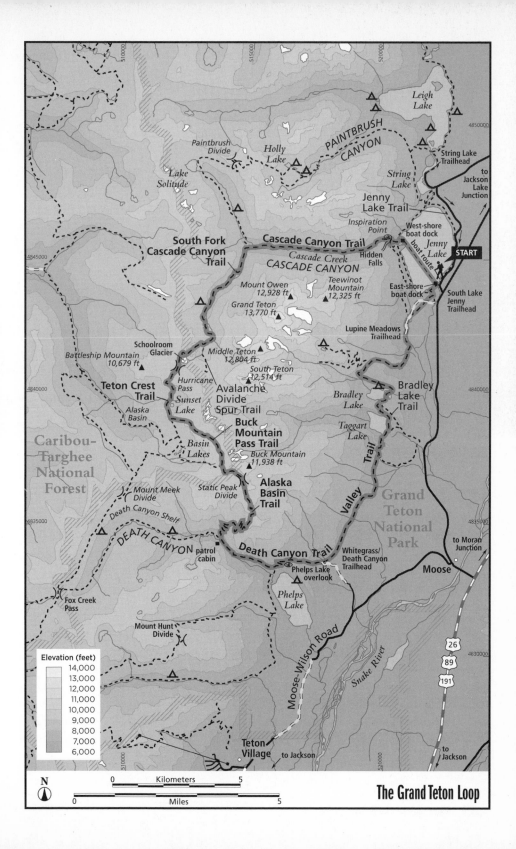

The Grand Teton Loop

Taking a lunch break on Buck Mountain Pass.

night out. In this case, go right (south) and then left (east) at the junction just before the lakes. Both routes take you to Buck Mountain Pass and are about the same length, but the Basin Lakes route involves a slightly tougher climb.

When you get to Buck Mountain Pass, you may have the impression that it's all downhill from here. That would be true if you were on Hurricane Pass going the other way, but not so this way. You still have a mild climb ahead of you to get to Static Peak Divide, the third pass on this route.

The trip up Static Peak Divide and the divide itself can get your adrenaline flowing. For a short stretch you hike on a trail gouged out of a steep cliff, so be careful. If you have young children with you, this would be a good place to keep them on a short leash. Static Peak Divide is quite austere and ruggedly spectacular, but don't get caught in a lightning storm.

From the divide, it's a nice high-country hike for about a mile, and then you drop into the forested south slope of Death Canyon. The trail switchbacks endlessly down to the floor of Death Canyon, the junction with the Death Canyon Trail, and a patrol cabin.

Go left (east), and continue your downhill hike on a fairly rocky trail down Death Canyon. You can see Phelps Lake ahead, which will probably be your next campsite. If so, go right (east) at the junction above the lake. About 0.4 mile later as you approach the shore of the lake, watch for a spur trail to the left (north) going around to the campsites on the north shore of the lake.

After your stay at Phelps Lake, retrace your steps back up to the Valley Trail above the lake and take a right (north). There is a surprising steep hill coming out of Phelps Lake, but this is somewhat indicative of the rest of this last day. As you go from Phelps Lake to Taggart Lake to Bradley Lake to the Lupine Meadows Trailhead, you climb a ridge (actually a moraine) between each point—nothing very steep, but constantly up and down.

This last day, hiking along the base of the Teton Range, is quite the contrast to the first three days of the hike spent in the high country. You go through mature forest with a few aspen groves and meadows. Watch for moose, black bears, and other wildlife, especially around Phelps Lake, where I also saw a rare rubber boa on the trail.

About 2 miles after Phelps Lake, go left (north) at the junction with the trail to the Death Canyon Trailhead. Also take left turns at the Beaver Creek, Taggart Lake, and Bradley Lake junctions. Glaciers created these three lakes by flowing out of the canyons, melting and leaving a moraine to form a natural dam. The view from Taggart Lake with Grand Teton as a backdrop is a great candidate for a postcard. Refer to the Valley Trail, Taggart Lake, and Bradley Lake trail descriptions for more information on this leg of your trip.

After Bradley Lake, you reach the junction with the trail to Garnet Canyon and Surprise and Amphitheater lakes. Go right (north), and hike the last 1.7 miles to the Lupine Meadows Trailhead. Walk about a mile over to the South Jenny Lake area where you left your vehicle to take the boat ride four days earlier.

Key Points

0.2 Junction with Jenny Lake Trail; go straight onto Cascade Canyon Trail.

0.5 Hidden Falls and junction with spur trail to Hidden Falls Overlook.

0.9 Inspiration Point.

1.6 Horse bypass trail.

4.9 Junction with South Fork and North Fork Cascade Canyon Trails; turn left.

8.4 Junction with spur trail to Avalanche Divide; turn right.

10.0 Hurricane Pass, Schoolroom Glacier, and the park boundary.

11.7 Sunset Lake.

12.0 Junction with Buck Mountain Pass Trail; turn left.

13.8 Junction with Alaska Basin Trail; turn left.

14.4 Buck Mountain Pass and the park boundary.

15.2 Static Peak Divide.

19.2 Junction with Death Canyon Trail; turn left.

21.4 Junction spur trail to Phelps Lake (trip to lake not included in mileage).

21.8 Phelps Lake Overlook.

23.0 Junction with trail to Death Canyon Trailhead; turn left.

26.7 Junction with Beaver Creek Trail; turn left.

27.5 Taggart Lake.

27.6 Junction with Taggart Lake Trail; turn left.

28.6 Bradley Lake.

28.7 Junction with Bradley Lake Trail; turn left.

30.0 Junction with Surprise Lake Trail; turn right.

31.7 Lupine Meadows Trailhead.

32.7 South Jenny Lake Trailhead.

Suggested itinerary:

First night: Lower section of South Fork Cascade Canyon.

Second night: Basin Lakes area in Alaska Basin.

Third night: Phelps Lake.

Options: I have never hiked up from Death Canyon to the Static Peak Divide, but while hiking down it I was left with the impression that I didn't want to do this trip in reverse. You have the option of shortening your trip by leaving vehicles at the Death Canyon or Taggart Lake Trailheads.

You could lengthen your trip by one day by spending a night on the Death Canyon Shelf. If this interests you, keep going south from Basin Lakes until you find one of many five-star campsites on the shelf. Then, the next morning, go back to Alaska Basin and on to Buck Mountain Pass and the rest of the trip.

If the Phelps Lake campsites are taken, you can camp in the Death Canyon Camping Zone above the patrol cabin at the junction of the Static Peak Trail. This adds 2 to 3 miles to the trip. This leaves a very long last day if you go all the way to Lupine Meadows, but you can also spend a night at the Bradley Lake campsite reserved just for hikers doing this loop.

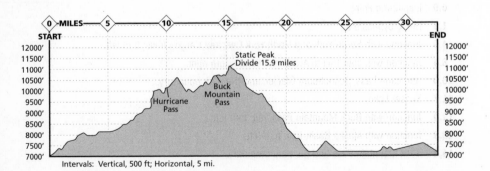

Intervals: Vertical, 500 ft; Horizontal, 5 mi.

Hiking down from Hurricane Pass into Alaska Basin with Sunset Lake in the background.

It's difficult to get the spacing correct on the last section of this trip, and it's easy to end up with more miles in one day than you really want. One option is to hang packs somewhere near the Death Canyon Trailhead and walk the rest of the trip with a daypack. If you do this, be sure to hang your packs out of reach of bears. Then, after reaching the Lupine Meadows Trailhead, drive back to the Death Canyon Trailhead for your overnight packs.

Side trip: You'll really miss something if you don't do the side trip up to Avalanche Divide, but it's a difficult climb to get there, making it for the fit and energetic only. If you have extra time after setting up camp in Alaska Basin, there are several short trails for other interesting side trips. In addition, the basin is open, subalpine country, which makes off-trail hiking easy.

Camping: The South Fork Camping Zone has at least fifteen campsites that are indicated, but you can camp anywhere, all the way up to a great site at the junction with the Avalanche Divide Trail. Most indicated campsites are four-star or five-star with nice views and privacy and good access to water, but shy away from any of the exposed sites if the weather looks ominous. Keep in mind that you aren't required to camp at the indicated sites. To keep the distance fairly equitable each day of your trip, camp in the lower part of this camping zone.

Alaska Basin is outside of the park in the Jedediah Smith Wilderness, so you can set up a no-trace camp anywhere in the basin. If you camp at Sunset Lake, don't camp on the shoreline. There are several great campsites safely away from the beautiful but fragile alpine lake.

Phelps Lake has three excellent designated campsites. As you approach the lake, watch for a junction with a trail going to the left (north) to the campsites. All of them are on the north shore of the lake with a terrific view of the lake, fire pits, room for two tents, and a shared bear box. The campsites are out of sight of the main trail, but the three campsites are fairly close, so please talk softly to respect the privacy of others.

Colter Bay and the Jackson Lake Lodge Area

21 Lakeshore Trail

This hike is a great choice for an evening or early-morning stroll, especially for campers staying in the Colter Bay area or for families with kids, who can help fill up Jackson Lake by throwing countless stones into it. It's a short, flat walk along the scenic shoreline of Colter Bay and Jackson Lake.

Start: Colter Bay Visitor Center.
Distance: 2.0-mile loop.
Difficulty: Easy.
Seasons: June through September.
Maps: Earthwalk Press Grand Teton map, National Park Service handout map, and

Grand Teton Natural History Association's Colter Bay brochure.
Trail contact: Grand Teton National Park, P.O. Drawer 170, Moose, WY 83012; (307) 739-3309; www.nps.gov/grte/.

Colter Bay and Mount Moran.

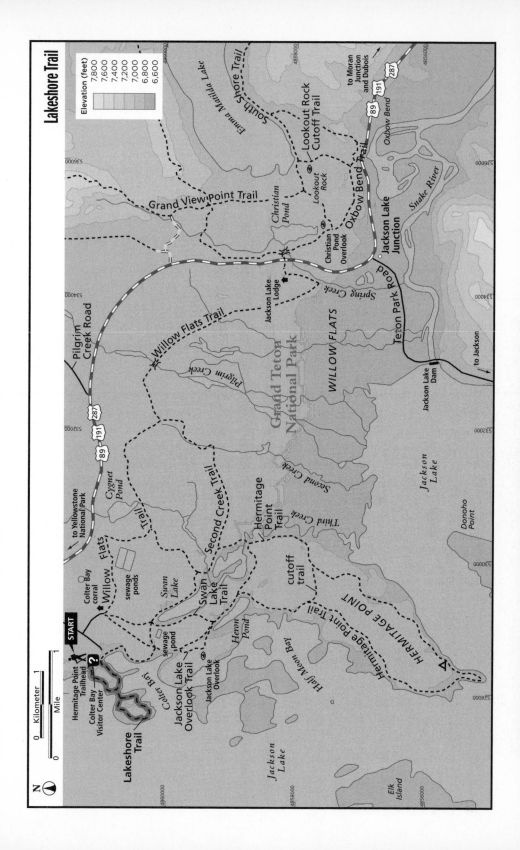

Finding the trailhead: Go 11 miles south of the northern park boundary on U.S. Highway 89 or drive 5.2 miles north of the Jackson Lake Junction and turn west into the Colter Bay area. After turning off the main highway, go 0.7 mile to the visitor center, taking the first right turn after passing the general store. Park at the visitor center, which has restrooms, and you'll find a general store a short walk east of the visitor center.

The Hike

The route starts out as a paved service road (no vehicles allowed) through the boat dock area and then turns into a well-used, singletrack trail. About one-tenth of a mile after the road ends, you reach a trail sign and then a dike across a narrow section of land out into a small island. The dike forms the center of this figure-eight route.

The trail circles the island (actually a small peninsula in Colter Bay), staying close to the water most of the way. Several beach areas invite you to stop and soak in the scenery of the Teton Range, especially Mount Moran, across the vast surface of Jackson Lake.

When you reach the bridge again, turn left and finish the figure-eight route. You come out by a park service amphitheater where rangers give talks. Check at the visitor center for a schedule.

Key Points

- **0.3** End of paved road.
- **0.4** Dike at center of figure-eight route.
- **1.5** Cross dike again.
- **1.9** Amphitheater.
- **2.0** Visitor center.

Options: The figure-eight loop can be done in either direction with no increase in difficulty.

Camping: No camping is allowed on this route.

22 Christian Pond

Christian Pond is a small lake mostly covered with pond lilies and other vegetation. It usually hosts nesting trumpeter swans that you can view safely from an overlook.

Start: Jackson Lake Lodge corral.
Distance: 1.2 miles out and back.
Difficulty: Easy.
Seasons: June through September.
Maps: Earthwalk Press Grand Teton map, National Park Service handout map, and

Grand Teton Natural History Association's Colter Bay brochure.
Trail contact: Grand Teton National Park, P.O. Drawer 170, Moose, WY 83012; (307) 739-3309; www.nps.gov/grte/.

Finding the trailhead: Take U.S. Highway 89 15.2 miles south of the north boundary of the park and turn right (west) or go 1 mile north of the Jackson Lake Junction and turn left (west) to Jackson Lake Lodge. Follow the signs and park in the corral parking lot or in the main lot for Jackson Lake Lodge, where you'll find restaurants, gift shops, and restrooms.

The Hike

Take the very heavily used trail from the corral under the highway underpass. Large trail riding groups leave regularly from here, so plan on seeing lots of horses and being careful where you step.

The trail immediately goes under the highway underpass, and just past it you reach a trail junction. If you take the loop option, you'll return to this junction. Go right (east), and hike another 0.4 mile through open country to the Christian Pond Overlook. Spend some time reading the interpretive signs and studying the swans and other waterfowl on Christian Pond before retracing your steps to Jackson Lake Lodge.

Options: If 1.2 miles isn't enough hiking for you, this trip can be extended to 3.1 miles by continuing past Christian Pond, turning left (north) on the Grand View Point Trail, and taking another left (west) 1.4 miles later. This takes you back to the junction just east of the highway overpass.

Camping: No camping is allowed on this route.

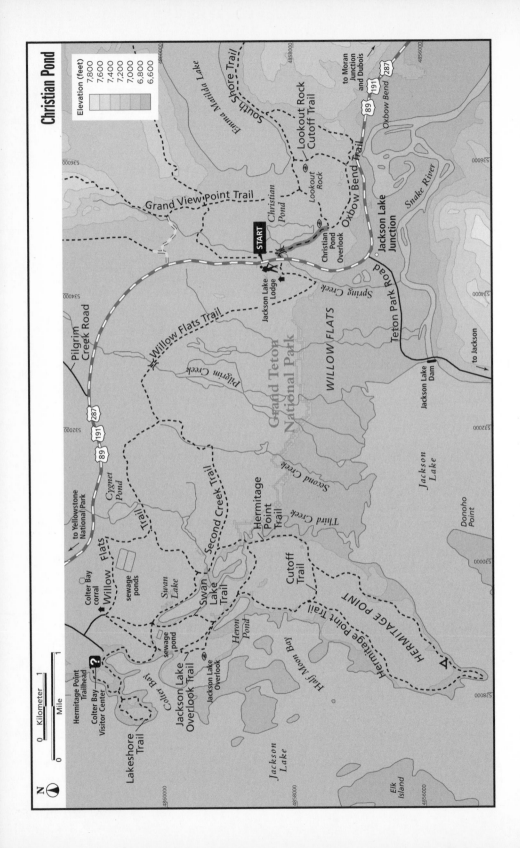

Christian Pond

Elevation (feet)
- 7,800
- 7,600
- 7,400
- 7,200
- 7,000
- 6,800
- 6,600

N

Kilometer 0 1
Mile 0 1

START

Christian Pond

Christian Pond Overlook

Grand View Point Trail

South Shore Trail

Emma Matilda Lake

Lookout Rock Cutoff Trail

Lookout Rock

Oxbow Bend Trail

Oxbow Bend

to Moran Junction and Dubois

287 191 89

Jackson Lake Junction

Snake River

Jackson Lake Lodge

Spring Creek

Teton Park Road

WILLOW FLATS

Grand Teton National Park

to Jackson

Jackson Lake Dam

Willow Flats Trail

Pilgrim Creek Road

287 191 89

to Yellowstone National Park

Cygnet Pond

Willow Flats Trail

Colter Bay corral

sewage ponds

Swan Lake

Second Creek Trail

Swan Lake Trail

Hermitage Point Trail

Second Creek

Third Creek

Jackson Lake

Donoho Point

HERMITAGE POINT

Cutoff Trail

Heron Pond

Half Moon Bay

Hermitage Point Trail

sewage pond

Jackson Lake Overlook Trail

Jackson Lake Overlook

Colter Bay

Lakeshore Trail

Colter Bay Visitor Center

Hermitage Point Trailhead

Jackson Lake

Elk Island

Pilgrim Creek

23 Swan Lake and Heron Pond

An easy circuit with special treats for wildlife watchers. Be sure to take a map and plan on closely noting the directional signs along the route. There are several junctions along this short loop, and if you're enjoying the scenery too thoroughly (which would be easy), you might get on the wrong trail.

Start: Hermitage Point Trailhead.
Distance: 3.0-mile "lollipop" loop.
Difficulty: Easy.
Seasons: Mid-June through September.
Maps: Earthwalk Press Grand Teton map, National Park Service handout map, and

Grand Teton Natural History Association's Colter Bay brochure.
Trail contact: Grand Teton National Park, P.O. Drawer 170, Moose, WY 83012; (307) 739-3309; www.nps.gov/grte/.

Finding the trailhead: Take U.S. Highway 89 into the park and turn west into the Colter Bay area, which is 11 miles south of the park's north boundary or 5.2 miles north of the Jackson Lake Junction with U.S. Highway 287. After turning into Colter Bay from the main highway, drive 0.9 mile on a paved road, then turn left (south) at the first turn after passing the general store. The trailhead is a little hard to find the first time you go into the Colter Bay area. It's located at the southern end of the big parking lot near the boat launch. Park here, along with the boaters. Be careful not to take the trail heading off to the east behind the trailhead sign. Instead, walk to the end of the parking lot toward the boat launch where you see trailhead signs marking the beginning of the trail. Go to the visitor center (just north of the trailhead) for toilet facilities.

The Hike

The trail starts out as a service road (with a locked gate and only occasionally used by vehicles). Along this stretch of trail, you can enjoy outstanding views of Colter Bay with Mount Moran providing a classic backdrop.

At the end of the dirt road, you reach Swan Lake Trail, the first junction where the loop section of this trip begins. Go right (south), unless you decide to take the route in reverse. The trail turns into a well-used singletrack, but it is still in excellent shape.

About 0.2 mile later, you reach a fork in the trail. If you don't mind a little hill, go right for a nice view from the Jackson Lake Overlook. Either trail takes you to Heron Pond about a half mile later.

Heron Pond is mostly covered with pond lilies. You can usually see pelicans, Canada geese, and other waterfowl species on the pond. In the evening hours, you might see beavers dining on the pond lilies or a moose in the willows surrounding the pond.

At the south end of Heron Pond, you reach a four-way trail junction. Take the sharpest left turn and head up a small hill toward Swan Lake.

Heron Pond and Mount Moran.

Like Heron Pond, Swan Lake is covered with yellow pond lilies. The lake gets its name from the same two trumpeter swans that have lived here since the 1980s. These rare swans have never produced any young, but they have fiercely defended their territory, chasing away other swans that otherwise might have successfully nested in this prime habitat.

After the lake, you pass by abandoned sewage ponds and then reach a junction with a trail heading off to the right (north) to the Colter Bay corral. Go left (west). Rejoin the abandoned service road 0.1 mile later for a 0.4-mile walk back to the trailhead.

Key Points

0.4   Junction with Swan Lake Trail; turn right.

0.6   Junction with Jackson Lake Overlook Trail, alternate route; turn right.

0.9   Jackson Lake Overlook Trail rejoins main trail.

1.0   Heron Pond.

1.4   Four-way junction; turn sharp left.

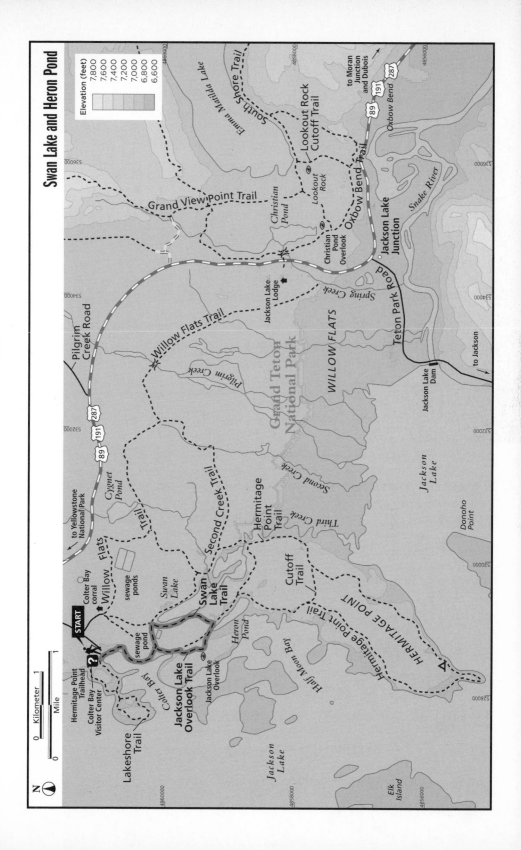

Swan Lake and Heron Pond

2.1 Swan Lake.

2.5 Junction with trail to corral; turn left.

2.6 Rejoin main trail to Colter Bay area; turn right.

3.0 Hermitage Point Trailhead.

Options: This loop can be taken in reverse with no increase in difficulty.

Side trip: If you want a longer hike, you can add to your day by hiking down to Hermitage Point.

Camping: No camping is allowed along this route.

24 Willow Flats Shuttle

This easy walk through a wildlife-rich flatland is a great hike for people staying at Jackson Lake Lodge or Colter Bay, but pick a cool day because the route goes through open meadows and willow flats with little shade along the way. Unlike trails in the high canyons of the Teton Range, snow leaves this area earlier in the spring and usually doesn't come as soon in the fall, which makes this route ideal for spring or fall hiking.

As far as shuttle hikes go, this is one of the easiest. It's only a short drive from Jackson Lake Lodge to leave your vehicle at the Colter Bay corral. You can also leave the vehicle in the Colter Bay parking area, but that is about 0.4 mile farther.

Start: Jackson Lake Lodge.
Distance: 4.9-mile shuttle.
Difficulty: Easy.
Seasons: June through September.
Maps: Earthwalk Press Grand Teton map, National Park Service handout map, and

Grand Teton Natural History Association's Colter Bay brochure.
Trail contact: Grand Teton National Park, P.O. Drawer 170, Moose, WY 83012; (307) 739-3309; www.nps.gov/grte/.

Finding the trailhead: Drive 15.2 miles south on U.S. Highway 89 south of the park boundary or 1 mile north of the Jackson Lake Junction with U.S. Highway 287, and turn west into the well-marked Jackson Lake Lodge area. The trail actually starts in a small parking area on the south side of the main lodge. Leave a vehicle or arrange to be picked up at the Colter Bay corral. Colter Bay is 4.2 miles northwest of Jackson Lake Lodge on US 89. After turning west into the Colter Bay area, follow the signs and park in the corral parking lot. Or, park in the Jackson Lake Lodge parking lot, use the restrooms, and enjoy the restaurants and gift shops in the lodge.

The Hike

The route starts right behind Jackson Lake Lodge on a mostly abandoned jeep road, which is closed to the public but used occasionally by concessionaires serving meals

Lily pads cover several lakes in the park.

for equestrian groups. Actually, the entire route is on a dirt road, but it's still a pleasant hike, especially for hikers who get nervous about being too far from civilization
and like perfectly flat hikes.

The first mile or so of the road goes through a large freshwater marsh. This is a
wildlife-rich area, so you stand a good chance of seeing coyotes, moose, sandhill
cranes, and other large wildlife species as well as a wealth of smaller birds. You go by
two classic beaver ponds and over Spring Creek on a bridge. You also get a great
view of the Teton Range across Jackson Lake along the first part of the hike.

After crossing the freshwater marsh, you go over Pilgrim Creek on a massive concrete bridge. Long ago, this was the main route into Jackson Hole. After US 89 was
constructed, this became a hiking trail with a monstrous, out-of-character bridge.

As you near the first junction, you enter a mixed-forest area dominated by a
stand of stately cottonwoods. When you reach the junction, take a right (northwest) and head toward Colter Bay. As you approach this junction, watch for a singletrack trail angling off to the right and cutting 200 yards off the trip when it
rejoins the road.

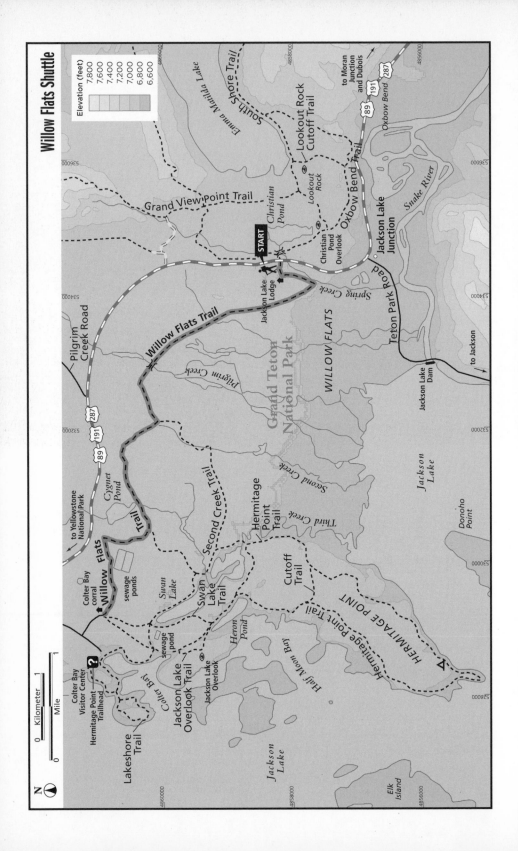

Mount Moran and Grand Teton from Willow Flats.

After the junction, the cottonwoods gradually give way to conifers. At the second junction, go right (north) to the corral.

Key Points

2.4 Junction with trail down Second Creek; turn right.
3.7 Junction with trail to Hermitage Point; turn right.
4.9 Colter Bay corral.

Options: This can be turned into a delightful "lollipop" loop hike. (Refer to the Willow Flats Loop description.) You can also start at Colter Bay instead of Jackson Lake Lodge with no increase in difficulty.

Camping: No camping is allowed along this route.

25 Lookout Rock

If you're looking for a short walk after dinner or for early morning during your stay at Jackson Lake Lodge, you couldn't do much better than this hike. You get a chance to see rare trumpeter swans nesting on Christian Pond, study the great Oxbow Bend of the Snake River, and enjoy a view of massive Emma Matilda Lake from Lookout Rock.

Start: Jackson Lake Lodge corral.
Distance: 3.8-mile "lollipop" loop.
Difficulty: Easy.
Seasons: Mid-June through September.
Maps: Earthwalk Press Grand Teton map, National Park Service handout map, and

Grand Teton Natural History Association Colter Bay brochure.
Trail contact: Grand Teton National Park, P.O. Drawer 170, Moose, WY 83012; (307) 739-3309; www.nps.gov/grte/.

Finding the trailhead: Take U.S. Highway 89 15.2 miles south of the north boundary of the park or 1 mile north of the Jackson Lake Junction and turn west to Jackson Lake Lodge. Follow the signs and park at the corral parking lot or the main lot at the lodge, where you'll find restaurants, gift shops, and restrooms.

The Hike

From the corral take the very heavily used trail from the corral and under the highway underpass. Large trail-riding groups regularly leave from here, so plan on seeing lots of horses and being careful where you step.

Just past the underpass, go right (southeast) at a junction and hike another 0.4 mile through open country to the Christian Pond Overlook. Spend some time reading the interpretive signs and studying the swans and other waterfowl commonly viewed on Christian Pond, then take the trail to the right (southeast) toward the Oxbow Bend of the Snake River.

This trail goes through the open sagebrush- and balsamroot-covered slope above U.S. Highway 287 and the Oxbow Bend of the Snake River. Take a few moments

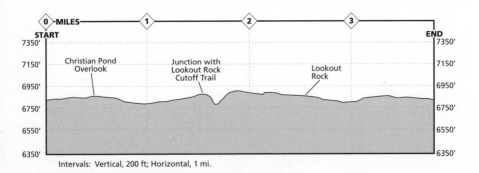

Intervals: Vertical, 200 ft; Horizontal, 1 mi.

Hiking the trail to Lookout Rock.

along the way to see how the Snake River has meandered severely and then cut through to create a small oxbow lake. You can often see pelicans and swans floating on the lake, even from a great distance. You also get a good view of Jackson Lake with the Teton Range as a dramatic backdrop and of Donoho Point Island.

After 0.9 mile you reach a junction with a cutoff trail to Lookout Rock. You can turn left and cut about a quarter mile off the trip, but I recommend continuing on the Oxbow Bend Trail. It's more scenic with less horse use. These two trails join the trail along the south shore of Emma Matilda Lake on each side of Lookout Rock.

Enjoy a rest and the vista from Lookout Rock Overlook before heading back toward Christian Pond. When you get to the Grand View Point Trail junction, go left (west) and go another 0.6 mile back to Christian Pond. Retrace your steps to Jackson Lake Lodge.

Key Points

0.2   Junction just past highway underpass.

0.6   Christian Pond Overlook and junction; turn right.

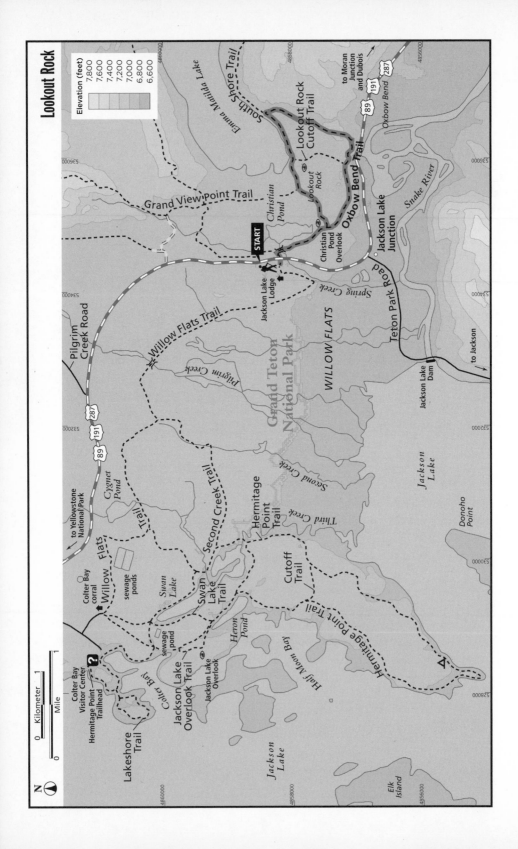

1.5   Junction with Lookout Rock Cutoff Trail; turn right.

2.3   Junction with South Shore Trail; turn left.

2.4   Lookout Rock and junction with cutoff trail; turn right.

2.6   Junction with Grand View Point Trail; turn left.

3.2   Christian Pond Overlook.

3.6   Junction with trail before underpass.

3.8   Jackson Lake Lodge corral.

Options: You can knock about a quarter mile off the hike by taking the Lookout Rock Cutoff Trail. You can also do this loop in reverse with no increased difficulty.

Camping: No camping is allowed on this route.

26 Willow Flats Loop

This moderate day hike through a scenic flatland not far from civilization makes a great hike for people staying at Jackson Lake Lodge. Pick a cool day though because the route goes through open meadows and willow flats with very little shade along the way. Unlike trails in the high canyons of the Teton Range, snow leaves this area earlier in the spring and usually doesn't come as soon in the fall, which makes this route ideal for spring or fall hiking.

Start: Jackson Lake Lodge.
Distance: 8.3-mile "lollipop" loop.
Difficulty: Moderate.
Seasons: June through September.
Maps: Earthwalk Press Grand Teton map, National Park Service handout map, and

Grand Teton Natural History Association's Colter Bay brochure.
Trail contact: Grand Teton National Park, P.O. Drawer 170, Moose, WY 83012; (307) 739-3309; www.nps.gov/grte/.

Finding the trailhead: Drive 15.2 miles south of the northern park boundary on U.S. Highway 89 or 1 mile north of the Jackson Lake Junction and turn west into the well-marked Jackson Lake Lodge area. The trail actually starts in a small parking area on the south side of the main lodge. Park in the Jackson Lake Lodge parking lot and use the restrooms and enjoy the restaurants and gift shops in the lodge.

The Hike

The route starts right behind Jackson Lake Lodge on a mostly abandoned jeep road, which is closed to the public but used occasionally by concessionaires serving meals for horse-riding groups. Actually, the entire route is on a dirt road, but it's still a pleasant hike, especially for hikers who get nervous about being too far from civilization and like perfectly flat hikes.

Outstanding scenery while hiking the Willow Flats Trail.

The first mile or so of the road goes through a large freshwater marsh. This is a wildlife-rich area, so you stand a good chance of seeing coyotes, moose, sandhill cranes, and other large wildlife species as well as a wealth of smaller birds. You go by two classic beaver ponds and over Spring Creek on a bridge. Along the first part of the hike, you also get a great view of the Teton Range across Jackson Lake.

Cross the freshwater marsh and hike over Pilgrim Creek on a massive concrete bridge. Long ago, this was the main route into Jackson Hole. After US 89 was constructed, this became a hiking trail with a monstrous, out-of-character bridge.

As you near the first junction, you enter a mixed-forest area dominated by a stand of stately cottonwoods. When you reach the junction, take a left (south) onto another road leading to a concessionaire-operated picnic area for clients from Jackson Lake Lodge. You get a great view of the Teton Range with Second Creek in the foreground.

After the picnic area, you (finally!) get on a singletrack trail through willow flats and grasslands. This trail is a little hard to find. It takes off to the right (west) about 100 yards before you reach the cooking area.

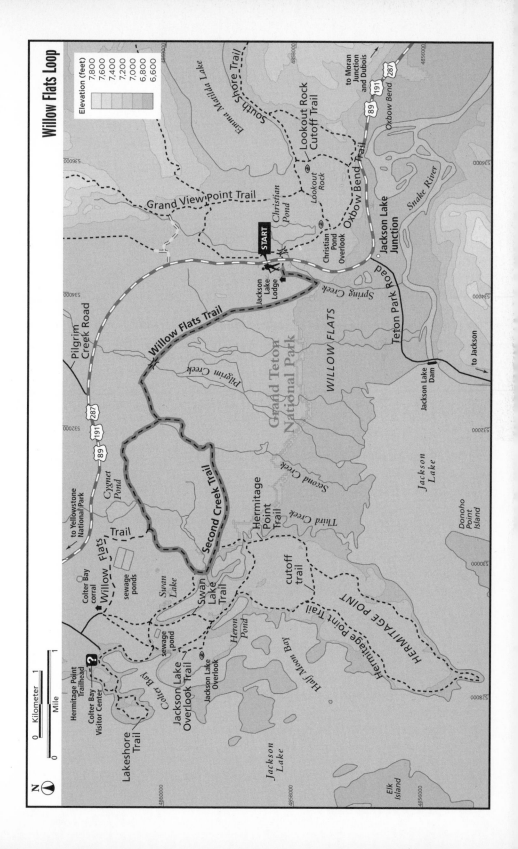

Willow Flats Loop

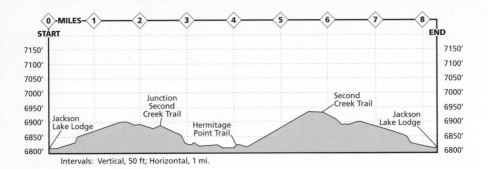

Intervals: Vertical, 50 ft; Horizontal, 1 mi.

When you find the trail, turn right (west) and follow it through a very scenic and unusual flatland for 0.9 mile to the next junction where you turn right (north) just before crossing Second Creek on a footbridge, again with a great view. From here, continue 0.6 mile along Second Creek until you reach the Willow Flats Trail between Jackson Lake Lodge and Colter Bay. Turn right (east), and go 1.3 miles to the next junction, which marks the end of the loop section of the trail. Along this stretch conifers gradually give way to the stand of stately cottonwoods you hiked through earlier in the day. From this junction turn left (northeast) and retrace your steps to Jackson Lake Lodge.

Key Points

2.4 Junction with trail down Second Creek; turn left.

3.1 Concessionaire picnic area at Second Creek; turn right.

4.0 Junction with trail to Hermitage Point; turn right.

4.6 Junction with Willow Flats Trail; turn right.

5.9 Junction with trail down Second Creek; turn left.

8.3 Jackson Lake Lodge.

Options: This can be turned into a shorter shuttle (4.9 miles) between Jackson Lake Lodge and the Colter Bay corral. Refer to the Willow Flats Shuttle description. You can also take the loop section of this hike in reverse with no increase in difficulty.

Camping: No camping is allowed along this route.

27 Hermitage Point

The Hermitage Point area is a confusing labyrinth of trails. After hiking all of them, I recommend this route as among the best hikes in the park—it's a unique hike on an undeveloped peninsula in expansive Jackson Lake. This is essentially an extended version of the Swan Lake and Heron Pond hike.

Start: Hermitage Point Trailhead.
Distance: 9.4-mile "lollipop" loop.
Difficulty: Moderate.
Seasons: Mid-June through September.
Maps: Earthwalk Press Grand Teton map, National Park Service handout map, and a

Grand Teton Natural History Association's Colter Bay brochure.
Trail contact: Grand Teton National Park, P.O. Drawer 170, Moose, WY 83012; (307) 739-3309; www.nps.gov/grte/.

Finding the trailhead: Take U.S. Highway 89 into the park and turn west into the Colter Bay area, which is 11 miles south of the park's north boundary or 5.2 miles north of the Jackson Lake Junction with U.S. Highway 287. After turning into Colter Bay from the main highway, drive 0.9 mile on a paved road, then turn left (south) at the first turn after passing the general store. The trailhead is a little hard to find the first time you go into Colter Bay. It's located at the south end of the big parking lot near the boat launch. Park here along with the boaters. Be careful not to take the trail heading off to the east right behind the trailhead sign. Instead, walk to the end of the parking lot toward the boat launch where you will see the trailhead signs marking the beginning of the trail. Go to the visitor center (just north of the trailhead) for restrooms.

The Hike

Be sure to take a map and plan on closely noting the directional signs along the route. There are several junctions along this short loop, and if you're enjoying the scenery too thoroughly (which would be easy), you might get on the wrong trail.

The trail starts out as a service road (with a locked gate and only occasionally used by vehicles). Along this stretch of trail, you can enjoy outstanding views of Colter Bay with Mount Moran providing a classic backdrop.

At the end of the dirt road, you reach the first junction where the loop section of this trip begins. Go right (south), unless you decide to take the route in reverse. The trail goes back to singletrack, but it's still in excellent shape.

About two-tenths of a mile later, you reach a fork in the trail. If you don't mind a little hill, go right for a nice view from the Jackson Lake Overlook. Either trail takes you to Heron Pond about a half mile later.

Heron Pond is mostly covered with pond lilies. You can usually see pelicans, Canada geese, and other waterfowl species on the pond. In the evening hours, you might see beavers dining on the pond lilies, and you might see a moose in the willows surrounding the pond.

Hiking back to Colter Bay on the east side of Hermitage Point.

At the south end of Heron Pond, you reach a four-way trail junction. Take the extreme right turn, and keep heading south along the lakeshore. You return to this junction later in the hike. In 0.8 mile, turn right (south) again at the junction with the cutoff trail.

After leaving Heron Pond, the trail stays out of sight of Jackson Lake for a while and then enters an open sagebrush flat with stunning views of the Teton Range, especially Mount Moran, across Hermitage Point. It stays this way for about a mile to the point.

After a rest to enjoy the scenery at the point, continue through the sagebrush meadows as you head back along the east side of the peninsula, past campsite 9, to the junction with the cutoff trail. Go right (north) at this junction, and hike another 0.7 mile to the second cutoff trail. Take a left (west). Go over a small hill and down to the four-way junction at the south end of Heron Pond. Take the first right (not the trail along the shore of Heron Pond) and go north back over the small ridge down to Swan Lake.

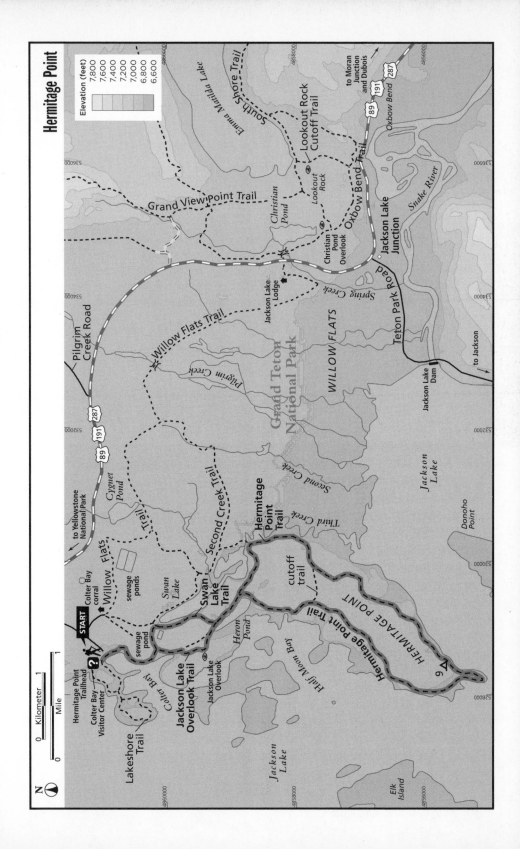

Like Heron Pond, Swan Lake is covered with yellow pond lilies. The lake gets its name from the same two trumpeter swans that have lived here since the 1980s. These rare swans have never produced any young, but they have fiercely defended their territory, chasing away other swans that otherwise might have successfully nested in this prime habitat.

After the lake, you pass by abandoned sewage ponds and then reach a junction with a trail heading off to the right (north) to the Colter Bay corral. Go left (west) and rejoin the abandoned service road 0.1 mile later for a 0.4-mile walk back to the trailhead.

Key Points

0.4 Junction with Swan Lake Trail; turn right.

0.6 Junction with Jackson Lake Overlook Trail (alternate route); turn right.

0.9 Rejoin main trail.

1.0 Heron Pond.

1.4 Four-way junction; turn far right.

2.2 Junction with cutoff trail; turn right.

4.4 Hermitage Point.

4.9 Designated campsite 9.

6.6 Junction with cutoff trail; turn right.

7.3 Junction with trail to Heron Pond; turn left.

7.8 Heron Pond and four-way junction; turn far right.

8.3 Swan Lake.

8.9 Junction with trail to Colter Bay corral; turn left.

9.0 Rejoin main trail to Colter Bay area.

9.4 Hermitage Point Trailhead.

Options: This route has many options—so many, in fact, that it can get confusing. You can take the cutoff trail to knock 4.4 miles off the trip, but you miss outstanding scenery from Hermitage Point. You can also go north at the second cutoff trail, but you miss Swan Lake.

Camping: You can camp on Hermitage Point at campsite 9—definitely a five-star campsite with a terrific view from a nice food area. There is room for three or four tents and easy access to water. Campfires are allowed in the designated fire pit.

◀ *Taking a break on Hermitage Point.*

28 Grand View Point

This is a wonderful short hike, but you have a serious hill to climb to earn the spectacular view from Grand View Point.

Start: Grand View Point Trailhead.
Distance: 2.2 miles out and back with loop option.
Difficulty: Easy.
Seasons: July through September.
Maps: Earthwalk Press Grand Teton map,

National Park Service handout map, and Grand Teton Natural History Association's Colter Bay brochure.
Trail contact: Grand Teton National Park, P.O. Drawer 170, Moose, WY 83012; (307) 739-3309; www.nps.gov/grte/.

Finding the trailhead: Drive 0.9 mile north of the Jackson Lake Lodge turnoff on U.S. Highway 89 and turn right (east) on an unpaved road. When I hiked this trip, this turnoff was unmarked, but it's the first right turn north of Jackson Lake Lodge. This is a rough jeep road for high-clearance vehicles only. Drive 0.8 mile up this jeep road until it ends at the trailhead. If you have a high-clearance vehicle, park right at the trailhead. If not, park in one of the turnouts along the first part of the jeep road and walk up the road to the trailhead. No trailhead facilities.

The Hike

Just uphill from the trailhead (0.2 mile), you come to a junction with a trail heading south toward Emma Matilda Lake. Go left (north) and start a gradual climb up to the top of Grand View Point. Just before you reach Grand View Point, you level off at a high point that could be confused with the real thing. Walk slightly farther down the trail for the real Grand View Point.

From the top of 7,586-foot Grand View Point, you get the view you expected, an outstanding look at Mount Moran and the rest of the mighty Teton Range off to the west, although this is partially obscured by trees. To our surprise, you also get a terrific sweeping vista of Two Ocean Lake and the lush meadows surrounding this huge mountain lake and, in the background, the Teton Wilderness. After a short rest, enjoy the downhill walk back to the trailhead.

Key Points

0.2 Junction with trail to Emma Matilda Lake; turn left.

1.1 Grandview Point.

Options: You can make a short loop out of this trip by continuing on the trail down the north side of Grand View Point for 0.9 mile to a junction

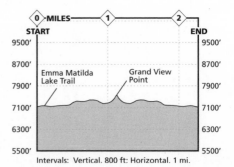

Intervals: Vertical. 800 ft: Horizontal. 1 mi.

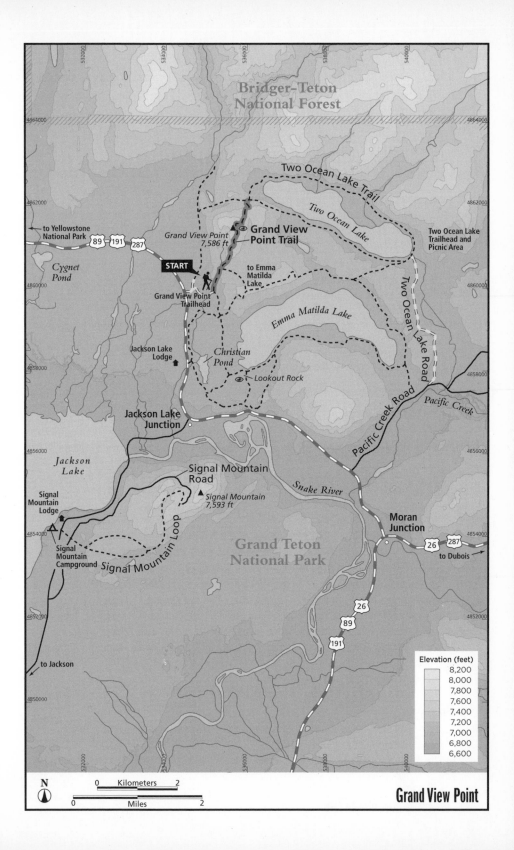

Bridger-Teton
National Forest

Two Ocean Lake Trail

Two Ocean Lake

Grand View Point
7,586 ft

**Grand View
Point Trail**

to Yellowstone
National Park

89 191 287

Two Ocean Lake
Trailhead and
Picnic Area

Cygnet
Pond

START

to Emma
Matilda
Lake

Grand View Point
Trailhead

Two Ocean Lake Road

Emma Matilda Lake

Jackson Lake
Lodge

Christian
Pond

Lookout Rock

Pacific Creek Road

Pacific Creek

**Jackson Lake
Junction**

Jackson
Lake

Snake River

**Signal Mountain
Road**

Signal Mountain
7,593 ft

Signal
Mountain
Lodge

Signal Mountain Loop

**Moran
Junction**

26 287

to Dubois

Signal
Mountain
Campground

**Grand Teton
National Park**

to Jackson

26

89

191

Elevation (feet)

8,200
8,000
7,800
7,600
7,400
7,200
7,000
6,800
6,600

N

0   Kilometers   2

0   Miles   2

Grand View Point

with the Pilgrim Creek Trail Go left (west) and hike 1.0 mile until you get into a large meadow where the trail turns into an abandoned jeep road. Walk down the jeep road a few hundred yards until you see another road heading off to the south. Go left and in 0.8 mile join the jeep road on which you drove to the trailhead. Turn left (east) and walk up the road to your vehicle. Total distance of the loop is 4.4 miles.

Side trip: You could hike down to the west end of Two Ocean Lake (2.6-mile round trip from Grand View Point) before heading back to the trailhead.

Camping: No camping is allowed along this route.

29 Two Ocean Lake

When I took this hike in late June, I didn't see another hiker, which is next to amazing considering how nice this hike is. The reason? When you think of hiking in Grand Teton, you don't think of gentle trails around forest-lined mountain lakes. Instead, you think about walking around the great peaks. Consequently, it appears, the northeast corner of the park has been spared the popularity of the western section of the park.

Start: Two Ocean Lake Trailhead and Picnic Area.
Distance: 6.4-mile loop.
Difficulty: Moderate.
Seasons: July through September.

Maps: Earthwalk Press Grand Teton map and National Park Service handout map.
Trail contact: Grand Teton National Park, P.O. Drawer 170, Moose, WY 83012; (307) 739-3309; www.nps.gov/grte/.

Finding the trailhead: From the Jackson Lake Junction, drive east on U.S. Highway 287 for 2.6 miles and turn left (north) on Pacific Creek Road. From the Moran Junction, drive west on US 287 for 1.2 miles and turn right (north) onto Pacific Creek Road. Drive 2.0 miles up Pacific Creek Road before turning left (west) on Two Ocean Road, which ends 2.4 miles later at the picnic area and trailhead. In the spring, heavy rains sometimes turn this road into a quagmire, and the park service closes it, so be sure to check the status of the road at an entrance station or visitor center before making the trip up Pacific Creek Road. The first part of Pacific Creek Road is paved, but it turns into a good gravel road. Two Ocean Road is also unpaved—and rougher than Pacific Creek Road. In good conditions, most vehicles can navigate both roads. Park at the trailhead, which has picnic tables and a pit toilet.

The Hike

You can take the loop from either direction. I liked the north shore better because it was more open, and the Teton Range could be viewed across the lake on the

Two Ocean Lake from the north-shore trail.

horizon. Since the morning is often more clear than the afternoon, you might try the north shore first.

Along the north shore, the Two Ocean Lake Trail splits several times. Take the high route, as the low route is for horses and has no footbridges over streams and marshy areas. Most of the north-shore trail goes through meadows with great scenery. The north-shore route is also slightly longer than that along the south shore. The south shore is more forested with fewer views of the lake, but it has a few large meadows.

Watch for waterfowl on the lake and moose in the thickets lining both shores. Also, and most important, stay alert for signs of the great bear, as grizzlies are more common in this area than in many parts of the park.

Key Points

3.3 Junction at the west end of the lake; turn left.
6.4 Two Ocean Picnic Area.

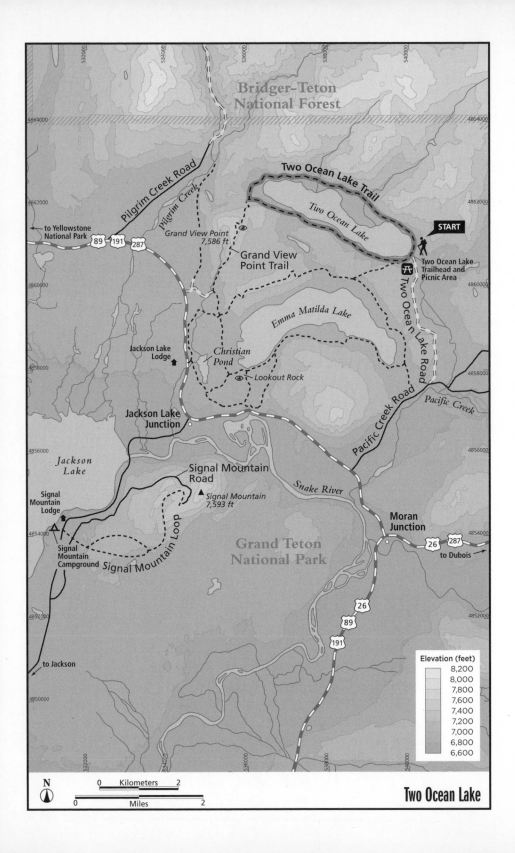

Two Ocean Lake

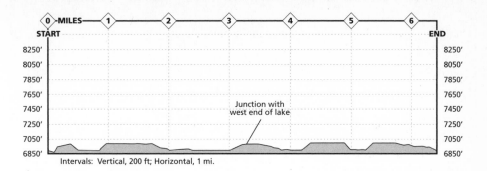

Intervals: Vertical, 200 ft; Horizontal, 1 mi.

Options: You can take this loop in either direction with no extra difficulty. You can also start this loop at the Grand View Point Trailhead, a good option in the spring if Two Ocean Road is closed.

Side trip: When you get to the west end of the lake, you can take a 2.6-mile trail (round trip) to the top of Grand View Point (see Hike 28) for a truly grand view of the lake you're hiking around. You can also take a 2-mile trail (round trip) from the picnic area to Emma Matilda Lake.

Camping: No camping is allowed along this route.

30 Signal Mountain

This is the only official hike in this part of the park with a unique view of Jackson Hole. From the top of Signal Mountain you get a panoramic view of the entire valley—Jackson Lake and the Teton Range to the west and Oxbow Bend of the Snake River to the north. Yes, you can drive to the top of Signal Mountain on a paved road, but you miss a great hike and some nice exercise if you do.

Start: Signal Mountain Lodge.
Distance: 7.4-mile "lollipop" loop.
Difficulty: Moderate.
Seasons: July through September.

Maps: Earthwalk Press Grand Teton map and National Park Service handout map.
Trail contact: Grand Teton National Park, P.O. Drawer 170, Moose, WY 83012; (307) 739-3309; www.nps.gov/grte/.

Finding the trailhead: Take U.S. Highway 89 north of Jackson for 11.5 miles and turn left (west) at the Moose Junction. Drive past the Moose Visitor Center (see Locator Map) and through the entrance station (about a mile after turning off the highway). Follow this paved park road for another 17 miles from the entrance station and turn left (west) into the Signal Mountain Lodge area. If you're coming from the north, drive 2.6 miles from the Jackson Lake Junction and turn right (west) at the Signal Mountain Lodge area.

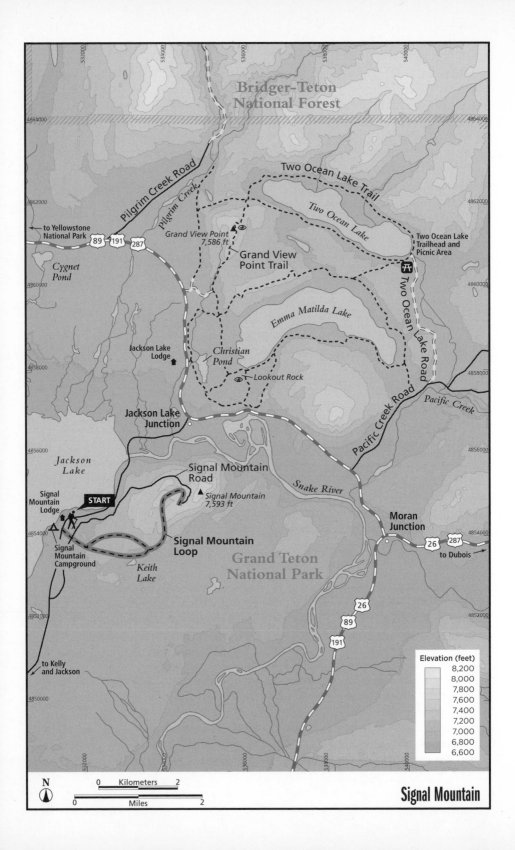

This trailhead is quite difficult to find. Actually, it's a small sign on the east side of the road about one-tenth of a mile south of the Signal Mountain Lodge turnoff. There is no place to pull off or park a car right at the trailhead, so it's easy to miss. You can also start this hike from the boat launch area, but again, no parking spots.

The closest place to park is in the large lot in the lodge area. This adds about 0.4 mile to the total distance of this trip. There are restrooms, a general store, a restaurant, gift shops, a gas station, and a ranger station in the Signal Mountain area.

The Hike

From the lodge area, carefully walk across the highway to the trail, where you climb gradually to the junction with the loop trail, which is about 0.3 mile after crossing (again, carefully) paved Signal Mountain Road.

When you get to the start of the loop trail, you can take a left (northeast) on the "ridge route" or a right on the "lake route." It makes no difference, but this trail description takes the clockwise route. This loop does not show on commercial maps for the area, but it is on the park service handout map.

The ridge route goes through mature forest and large sagebrush meadows. When you get halfway around the loop, you see the spur trail going to the top of the mountain. This is a must-see side trip and adds about a mile to the total distance of the trip. The view from the top is so much more rewarding when you walk up.

After you rejoin the loop trail, go left (south) and continue through a big meadow until you drop down to the more forested area around Keith Lake (watch for many species of waterfowl on the lake) and then back to the start of the loop. Go left (west), and retrace your steps to the lodge area. The trail is in great shape and easy to follow the entire way.

Commercial maps and the park service handout show a trail going from the top of the ridge north to Oxbow Bend, but this trail has been abandoned because of the unsafe condition of the old bridge over the Snake River.

Key Points (from Signal Mountain Lodge):

0.2 Trailhead on main park road.

0.4 Signal Mountain Summit Road.

Intervals: Vertical, 200 ft; Horizontal, 1 mi.

0.7	Start of loop trail; turn left.
3.2	Spur trail to top of Signal Mountain.
3.7	Summit of Signal Mountain.
4.2	Loop trail.
6.7	End of loop.
7.0	Signal Mountain Road.
7.2	Trailhead on main park road.
7.4	Signal Mountain Lodge area.

Options: If you don't like hills, you can, of course, get a ride to the top and walk down to the lodge.

Camping: No camping is allowed along this route.

31 Emma Matilda Lake

Emma Matilda and Two Ocean lakes offer a gentle beauty quite unlike the high peaks for which Grand Teton National Park is so well known. Even though you definitely get the feeling of being in the backcountry, these trails aren't even shown on the park service backcountry brochure. When I took this hike in late June, I didn't see another hiker on the entire circuit around the lake. This hike, like Two Ocean Lake to the north, is in the northeast corner of the park, which has been spared the popularity of the ultrapopular hikes up the canyons of the Teton Range. I hiked the north shore first in the morning because it is more open and offers great views of the Teton Range across the lake.

Start: Emma Matilda Trailhead.
Distance: 10.5-mile loop.
Difficulty: Moderate.
Seasons: July through September.
Maps: Earthwalk Press Grand Teton map and National Park Service handout map. Note:

Some maps do not show the trail around the west end of the lake, so refer to the park service handout map.

Trail contact: Grand Teton National Park, P.O. Drawer 170, Moose, WY 83012; (307) 739-3309; www.nps.gov/grte/.

Finding the trailhead: From the Jackson Lake Junction, drive east on U.S. Highway 287 for 2.6 miles and turn left (north) on Pacific Creek Road. From the Moran Junction, drive west on US 287 for 1.2 miles and turn right (north) onto Pacific Creek Road. From either direction, drive 1.5 miles up Pacific Creek Road and park at a turnout on the left (west). When we hiked this trail, there was no sign marking this trailhead. If you are coming from Jackson Lake Junction and you get to the Two Ocean Road turn, you have missed it, so backtrack 0.5 mile. The first part of Pacific Creek Road is paved, but it turns into a good gravel road suitable for most vehicles. Technically, the park service doesn't consider this an official trailhead, which is why it and the first

Emma Matilda Lake from Lookout Rock.

junction have no signs. Park at the trailhead, which has limited parking space. There are no trailhead facilities.

The Hike

From the trailhead, it's 0.5 mile to the junction with the loop trail around the lake. This junction is in a big meadow and was not signed when I was there. Several unofficial trails make it more confusing, so be alert to get on the correct trail. If you're following this trail description, go right (northwest) at this junction. Don't go extreme right and get on an unofficial trail, which takes you back to Pacific Creek Road.

After the junction, you face a small climb to get to the ridge above the lake. At 2.2 miles, turn left at the cutoff trail to Two Ocean Lake.

Most of the north-shore trail goes through sagebrush meadows, aspen stands, and a mixed-conifer forest, often offering up a nice view of the lake with the Teton Range as the backdrop. The smell of sage accompanies you most of the way. In the

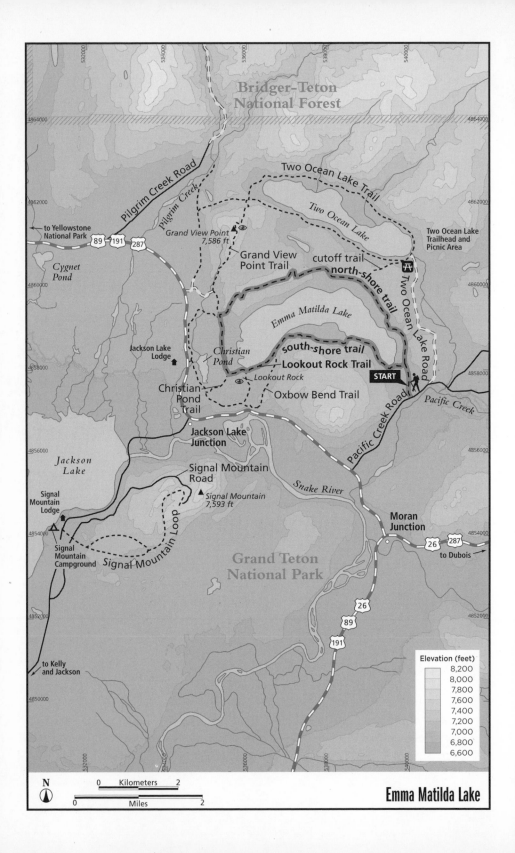

fall, the aspens turn the landscape gold, and in the spring the abundance of arrow-head balsamroot gives a yellow flair to the entire north shore. One section of the north shore is well into the natural process of recovering from a forest fire.

When you get to the Grand View Point Trail, go left (south) on a trail (not shown on some maps) along the west end of the lake. In 1.4 miles, you get to a confusing section of the trail. Stay alert between here and the Oxbow Bend Trail Junction. This is a triangular junction with the trail to Christian Pond and Jackson Lake Lodge. If you plan to take a short side trip to Christian Pond to see the swans or visit Jackson Lake Lodge before heading back to the trailhead, go right (west). If you aren't inter-ested in a side trip, go left (east). In the next 0.3 mile, two more trails join the main trail from the south. Go left (east) at both junctions. In other words, to stay on the main route, take left turns only.

Lookout Rock lies between the two junctions and is a great place to relax and have lunch. You get a better view of the lake from this overlook than from anywhere else on the forest-lined south-shore trail until you get near the west end of the lake when the forest opens up to reveal the big jewel of a lake called Emma Matilda. Unlike the openness of the north-shore trail, the mature forest of the south shore blocks the view of the lake, but this is still a great walk in the woods.

Just before you get to the junction where you started the loop, you cross a foot-bridge over the outlet of the lake. When I hiked this trail, the local beaver popula-tion had appropriated the bridge as a good base for a dam. Unfortunately, the dam was backing up the entire lake, so the trail crew had to go in later that summer and undo this ultra-ambitious beaver's dreams. From this junction, take a right (east) and walk the last half mile to the trailhead.

Key Points

0.5 Beginning of loop around Emma Matilda Lake.

2.2 Cutoff trail to Two Ocean Lake Picnic Area; turn left.

4.9 Junction with Grand View Point Trail; turn left.

6.3 Junction with Christian Pond Trail; turn left.

6.5 Junction with Lookout Rock Trail; turn left.

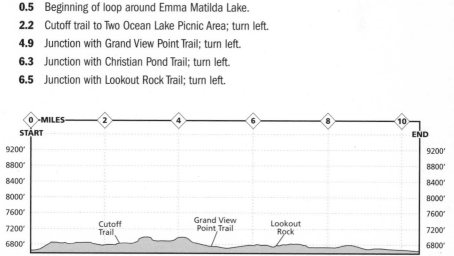

Intervals: Vertical, 400 ft; Horizontal, 2 mi.

6.6 Lookout Rock.

6.7 Junction with Oxbow Bend Trail; turn left.

10.0 End of loop around Emma Matilda Lake.

10.5 Emma Matilda Lake Trailhead.

Options: You can take this loop in either direction with no extra difficulty. You can also hike the loop around Emma Matilda Lake by starting at the Two Ocean Lake, Grand View Point, or Jackson Lake Lodge trailheads. For an unusual option, hike half the loop, go over to Jackson Lake Lodge for lunch, and hike back on the other side of the lake.

Side trip: When you get to the west end of the lake, you can take a 3.6-mile trail (round trip) to the top of Grand View Point for a great view of the Teton Range and Two Ocean Lake. You can also take a 2.0-mile (round trip) trail over to see Two Ocean Lake. Lastly, you can take the short side trip over to see nesting trumpeter swans at Christian Pond.

Camping: No camping is allowed along this route.

North Trails Area

32 Glade Creek

Most people don't think about this section of Grand Teton National Park, so you can plan on having Glade Creek and most of the north trails to yourself. This hike actually starts outside the park in the John D. Rockefeller Jr. Memorial Parkway, but the area is just as undeveloped as the park itself—in fact, more wild than many parts of the park. The trailhead sign says that it's 3.5 miles to the park boundary, but this is probably exaggerated by at least a half mile and perhaps more.

Start: Glade Creek Trailhead.
Distance: 7.0 miles out and back.
Difficulty: Easy.
Seasons: July through September.

Maps: Earthwalk Press Grand Teton map and National Park Service handout map.
Trail contact: Grand Teton National Park, P.O. Drawer 170, Moose, WY 83012; (307) 739-3309; www.nps.gov/grte/.

Coming into the big meadow where the Snake River flows into Jackson Lake, seen in the background.

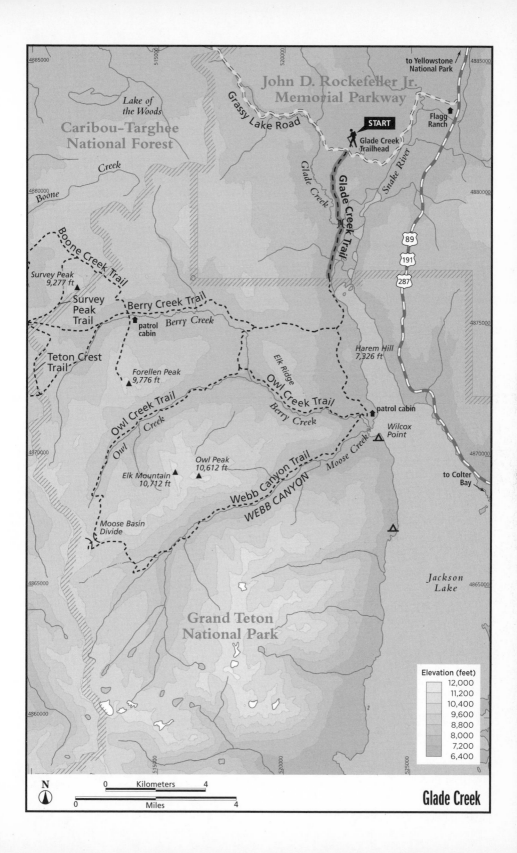

Glade Creek

Finding the trailhead: From U.S. Highway 89, drive 4.4 miles west of Flagg Ranch on Grassy Lake Road (also known as Ashton-Flagg Ranch Road) and park at the trailhead on the left (south) side of the road. Park in the small lot at the trailhead, which has a pit toilet.

The Hike

The trail starts out through a mature lodgepole forest. After about a mile and a half, you cross Glade Creek on a footbridge. Shortly thereafter, you drop down a fairly steep hill to a massive meadow. To the left, you can see the Snake River flowing into Jackson Lake and one of two huge freshwater marshes in the park. (The other is just south and west of Jackson Lake Lodge.) You can also see Jackson Lake off to the south. This is a wildlife-rich area, so take your time before retracing your steps to the trailhead. You may see some moose, swans, and other wildlife, especially in the early morning or near sunset. Even the mighty grizzly bear frequently roams through this rich habitat. But be forewarned: There is one wildlife species you will see and not enjoy. This is the only section of trail in the park where I had to stop and get out the mosquito repellent and netting.

Key Points

1.5 Cross the Glade Creek footbridge.

2.0 Break out into a big meadow.

3.5 Park boundary.

Side trip: If you set up camp, you can hike up Berry Creek or do the Elk Ridge Loop hike before heading back to the trailhead.

Camping: You may set up a no-trace camp anywhere along this route, before or after entering the park. You need a backcountry camping permit to camp in the park, but no permit is required for camping in the parkway.

33 Elk Ridge

This trail loops around forested Elk Ridge in the remote "north trails" section of Grand Teton National Park. It lacks the alpine vistas of many hikes such as nearby Moose Basin Divide and Jackass Pass, but it provides the quiet solitude of a walk in the woods with, most likely, only wild companions. You are not likely to see many hikers on this route, but you might see Old Ephraim, the grizzly bear. It's a long day hike or overnighter.

Start: Glade Creek Trailhead.
Distance: 19.3-mile "lollipop" loop.
Difficulty: Difficult day hike, moderate overnighter.
Seasons: July through September.

Maps: Earthwalk Press Grand Teton map and National Park Service handout map.
Trail contact: Grand Teton National Park, P.O. Drawer 170, Moose, WY 83012; (307) 739-3309, www.nps.gov/grte/.

Finding the trailhead: From U.S. Highway 89, drive 4.4 miles west of Flagg Ranch on the Grassy Lake Road (also known as Ashton-Flagg Ranch Road) and park at the trailhead on the left (south) side of the road. Park in the small lot at the trailhead, which has a pit toilet.

The Hike

For details on the first section of this hike, refer to the Glade Creek trail description (Hike 32). About a half mile after crossing into the park, the trail leaves the meadow and climbs up onto the slopes of Harem Hill through a short section of mature forest before emerging into another huge mountain meadow. The trail follows the east side of the meadow until you see the junction with the Berry Creek Trail. Some older maps may show a triangle junction at this point, but the park service removed this in 1995.

When you reach the Berry Creek Trail junction, go right (west) and continue hiking through a series of big meadows until you see a junction with the cutoff trail to Owl Creek. Go left (south), and cross Berry Creek (sorry, no footbridge), then climb a small ridge above the creek and back down into the confluence of Berry

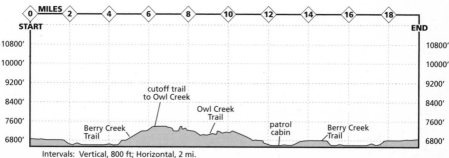

Intervals: Vertical, 800 ft; Horizontal, 2 mi.

Fording Berry Creek.

Creek and Owl Creek. At the junction, go left (east) and cross Berry Creek again just before it disappears into Owl Creek (sorry, again no footbridge).

If you're backpacking, the confluence area is a reasonably good point about halfway through this trip for your camp. You won't have trouble finding a great campsite in this area, which is at the east end of a huge meadow lining Owl Creek.

The trail gradually climbs up to a bench above Owl Creek and stays there until you drop down to a big, flat meadow on the shore of Jackson Lake. At the beginning of the meadow, go left (northeast) at the junction with the Webb Canyon Trail and left (north) again at the junction with the Glade Creek Trail at the patrol cabin.

It's about 2 scenic miles more (nice views of Jackson Lake) back to the junction with the Berry Creek Trail. Turn right (north) and retrace your steps to Glade Creek and the trailhead.

Key Points

1.5 Cross the Glade Creek footbridge.

2.0 Break out into a big meadow.

3.5 Park boundary.

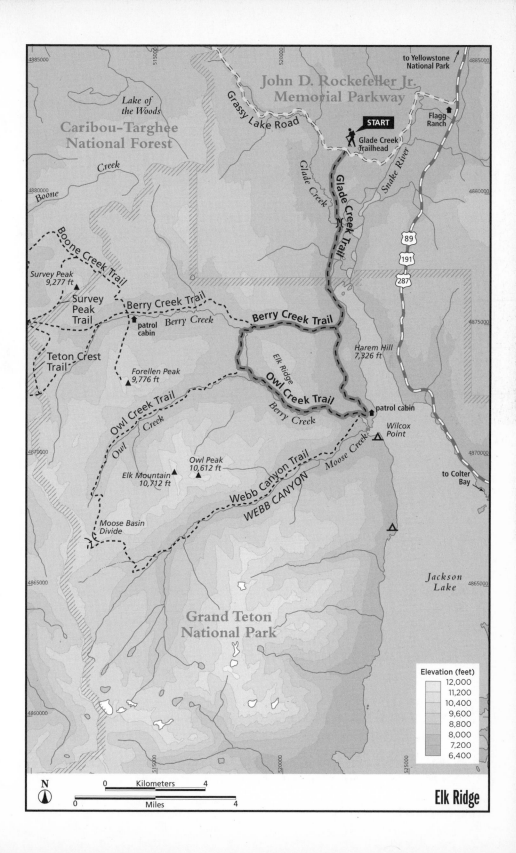

The striking openness of Lower Berry Creek.

4.9 Junction with Berry Creek Trail; turn right.

6.4 Junction with cutoff trail to Owl Creek; turn left.

8.4 Junction with Owl Creek Trail; turn left.

12.3 Junction with Webb Canyon Trail; turn left.

12.4 Patrol cabin and junction with Glade Creek Trail; turn left.

14.4 Junction with Berry Creek Trail; turn right.

15.9 Park boundary.

19.3 Glade Creek Trailhead.

Options: You can knock 9.8 miles off this trip by paddling a canoe from Leeks Marina on the east side of Jackson Lake over to Wilcox Point and doing only the 9.5-mile loop around Elk Ridge. This loop might be more difficult when done clockwise instead of counterclockwise as described because of a fairly big hill coming from the south on the 2-mile cutoff trail between Owl Creek and Berry Creek.

Side trip: If you're camping at Owl Creek, take a morning or evening stroll west on the trail along the stream and watch for wildlife.

Camping: You can set up a no-trace camp anywhere along this route, before or after entering the park. You need a permit when camping in the park.

34 Jackass Pass

Welcome to the "north trails," the forgotten section of Grand Teton National Park—and prepare to savor the solitude of this wilderness area. This is a more gentle and uncrowded part of the park but still exceptionally beautiful. I spent four days (including an August weekend) hiking the north trails and only saw one other group of hikers. This is a good choice for a long backpacking or base-camp trip into the most remote section of Grand Teton National Park.

Start: Glade Creek Trailhead.
Distance: 28.7 miles out and back with a small loop at the end.
Difficulty: Difficult.
Seasons: Mid-July through mid-September.

Maps: Earthwalk Press Grand Teton map and National Park Service handout map.
Trail contact: Grand Teton National Park, P.O. Drawer 170, Moose, WY 83012, (307) 739-3309, www.nps.gov/grte/.

Finding the trailhead: From U.S. Highway 89, drive 4.4 miles west of Flagg Ranch on Grassy Lake Road (also known as Ashton-Flagg Ranch Road) and park at the trailhead on the left (south) side of the road. Park in the small lot at the trailhead, which has a pit toilet.

The Hike

This hike actually starts outside of the park in the John D. Rockefeller Jr. Memorial Parkway, a 24,000-acre area that is just as undeveloped as the park itself—in fact, more wild than many parts of the park. The trailhead sign says that it's 3.5 miles to the park boundary, but this is probably exaggerated by at least a half mile and perhaps more.

The trail starts out through a mature lodgepole forest. After about a mile and a half, you cross Glade Creek on a footbridge. Shortly thereafter, you drop down a fairly steep hill into a massive meadow. To the left, you can see the Snake River as it flows into Jackson Lake and one of two large freshwater marshes found in the park. (The other is just south and west of Jackson Lake Lodge.) You can also see Jackson Lake off to the south, and you also may be able to see some moose, swans, and other wildlife, especially in the early morning or near sunset. Even the mighty grizzly bear frequently roams through this rich habitat. But be forewarned: There is one wildlife species you will see and not enjoy. This is the only section of trail in the park where I had to stop and get out the mosquito repellent and netting.

About a half mile after crossing into the park, the trail leaves the meadow and climbs up onto the slopes of Harem Hill through a short section of mature forest before emerging into another huge mountain meadow. The trail follows the east side of the meadow until you see the junction with the Berry Creek Trail. Some older maps may show a triangle junction at this point, but the park service removed this in 1995.

Upper Berry Creek, one huge meadow all the way to Jackass Pass.

Go right (west) and continue through a series of big meadows until you reach the junction with the cutoff trail going south over to Owl Creek. Go right (west) again, and continue up Berry Creek all the way to the base of Jackass Pass.

The trail up Berry Creek is one of the nicest in the park, probably the nicest that doesn't have any hikers on it. An immense, lush meadow lines Berry Creek all the way to the pass while Forellen and Survey Peaks supply the scenic backdrop. Watch for moose, elk, black bear, and, of course, Old Griz.

When you get to the junction with the trail veering off to the right and heading for the north side of Survey Peak, go left (west). If you decide to take the loop at the end of this trail, you'll be coming down that trail later in the day.

Shortly after this junction, you'll pass a patrol cabin off to the left and a sign for the trail up Forellen Peak. The Forellen Peak Trail receives low-priority maintenance, so it can be hard to find, especially in the lower, forested sections.

From the cabin, you start your steady climb up to the park boundary at 8,500-foot Jackass Pass. There are a few switchbacks on the steepest parts, but this is not really a difficult hill. The way up offers terrific views back down Berry Creek toward Jackson Lake. Unlike most passes and divides, however, Jackass Pass itself offers little scenery for the weary hiker. As the trail levels out and nears the pass, it slips into a lodgepole forest.

After a rest on the pass (or just before the pass if you want scenery), you have to make the decision whether to backtrack or try the loop trail around Survey Peak. If you choose the latter, as I did, continue past the pass to a junction with the Teton Crest Trail about a tenth of a mile down the trail. Go right (north), and hike along a flat bench with sweeping vistas of the Jedediah Smith Wilderness in the Targhee National Forest off to the west and Survey Peak to the east. This section of trail is outside the park, but it's as scenic as any trail in the park. The trail goes through an unusually huge, flat bench on the Teton Crest. The first part of this leg is forested, but about halfway to Boone Creek it opens up and stays that way. As you near Boone Creek and drop down a steep slope to the junction, the trail becomes a little vague in spots.

At the Boone Creek junction, go right (east) onto the Survey Peak Trail and hike through a treeless "high-country prairie" as you climb up to the north flank of Survey Peak. The first part of this trail up to the park boundary is easy to follow, probably kept distinct by horse parties and hunters. As you near the boundary, however, the trail becomes indistinct. Watch for cairns, and stay in the little valley, which heads up to 8,700-foot Survey Pass at the park boundary. This is great elk country, as witnessed by a huge wallow just inside the park.

The trail drops sharply down to Berry Creek. This section of trail is not well maintained and is difficult. Hopefully, you decided to camp down at Berry Creek and don't have your big pack on for this deadly downhill. You will be glad you did the loop clockwise and avoided this extremely steep climb.

When you reach the Berry Creek Trail, go left (east) and retrace your steps back to the Glade Creek Trailhead. I noticed that the miles went by much faster than expected, and I theorized that the mileage might be slightly overstated on the trail signs. As you near the trailhead, you'll notice the hill climbing up to Glade Creek from the Snake River. It doesn't seem that big coming down, but at the end of a three-day backpack, it seems much steeper.

Key Points

1.5 Cross the Glade Creek footbridge.

2.0 Break out into a big meadow.

3.5 Park boundary.

4.9 Berry Creek Trail; turn right.

6.5 Junction with cutoff trail to Owl Creek; turn right.

11.1 Junction with Survey Peak Trail; turn left.

11.5 Patrol cabin and junction and trail to Forellen Peak; turn right.

13.1 Jackass Pass.

13.2 Junction with Teton Crest Trail; turn right.

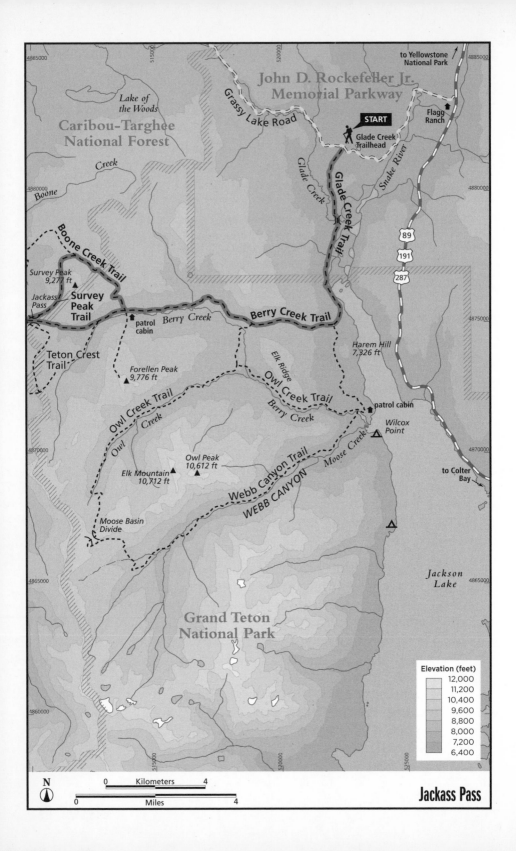

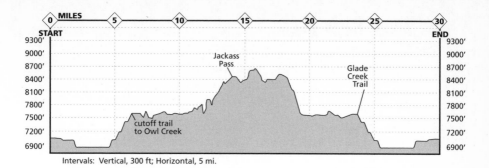

Intervals: Vertical, 300 ft; Horizontal, 5 mi.

15.4 Junction with Boone Creek Trail; turn right.

17.6 Junction with Berry Creek Trail; turn left.

22.3 Junction with cutoff trail to Owl Creek; turn left.

23.8 Junction with Glade Creek Trail; turn left.

25.2 Park boundary.

28.7 Glade Creek Trailhead.

Suggested itinerary: Set up a base camp in Lower Berry Creek and spend two or three nights there, exploring new sections of the park's north country each day, and then retracing your steps out to the Glade Creek Trailhead.

Options: Rather than carry your overnight pack to Jackass Pass, you can set up a base camp in Berry Creek and day hike the loop around Survey Peak.

Side trip: In addition to the loop around Survey Peak, you can hike south along the Teton Crest Trail from Jackass Pass, but this is an out-and-back side trip. If you set up a base camp in Berry Creek, you can hike up Berry Creek to Jackass Pass and Survey Peak, but you could take another day and go over to Owl Creek or hike the Elk Ridge Loop.

Camping: This is an open camping area, so you may set up a no-trace camp anywhere along this route, before or after entering the park, but be sure to get a permit for camping in the park. It won't be difficult to find scenic campsites, especially at Berry Creek. If you decide to carry your overnight pack around Survey Peak, you can camp anywhere along the Teton Crest, but water can be scarce late in the season in this high country.

35 Moose Basin Divide

This is a long backpacking trip into the most remote section of Grand Teton National Park.

Start: Glade Creek Trailhead.
Distance: 41.2-mile "lollipop" loop.
Difficulty: Difficult.
Seasons: Late July through mid-September.

Maps: Earthwalk Press Grand Teton map and National Park Service handout map.
Trail contact: Grand Teton National Park, P.O. Drawer 170, Moose, WY 83012; (307) 739–3309, www.nps.gov/grte/.

Finding the trailhead: Drive 4.4 miles west of Flagg Ranch on Grassy Lake Road (also known as Ashton–Flagg Ranch Road) and park at the trailhead on the left (south) side of the road. Park in the small lot at the trailhead, which has a pit toilet.

Moose Creek cascading through Webb Canyon.

Upper Moose Creek, about a mile from Moose Basin Divide.

The Hike

For the details on the first section of this hike from Glade Creek to Berry Creek, refer to the Jackass Pass (Hike 34) and Glade Creek (Hike 32) route descriptions.

At the junction with the Berry Creek Trail, go left (south) and continue to hike through a mature forest interspersed with huge meadows. The trail is in great shape all the way to the patrol cabin, and you get some nice views of Jackson Lake over the last mile or so before the cabin. It seems like a short 8 miles from Glade Creek to the patrol cabin.

At the junction in front of the patrol cabin, go right (west) and hike another 0.1 mile to the junction with the loop trail over Moose Basin Divide. If you're following this clockwise route, go left (south), and ford Berry Creek. Sorry, no footbridge means getting your feet wet just before setting up camp.

After Berry Creek, the trail goes through an open bench and then over into Moose Creek. This vicinity is a good choice for camping the first night out.

About a mile up the trail, you enter Webb Canyon, a steep and narrow section of the Moose Creek drainage, and stay there for several miles. The trail stays close to the stream most of the way, and Moose Creek is mighty impressive as it crescendos out of the high country. It's a constant cascade through the steep canyon. It almost makes you forget the big hill you're climbing.

After about 6 or 7 miles of canyon hiking, you break out into gorgeous subalpine country in Moose Basin. You can camp anywhere in the basin, and it will be a memorable night in paradise. When I was there, it was a monstrous "moose-less" meadow, but in most cases you should be able to see moose, elk, and other large wildlife in this rich high country, including the grizzly, so be alert.

From the basin, it's 2 to 3 miles to the divide. In the last 2 miles, the trail becomes a series of cairns in spots, and it's a wildflower carpet all the way. Actually, the hill is not that bad once you get to Moose Basin. Most of the serious climbing is behind you in Webb Canyon.

Save some water for lunch at the top. Late in the season, water is scarce for a mile or so on each side of the divide.

After a good rest on the 9,700-foot divide, drop down sharply toward upper Owl Creek and onto a bench covered with whitebark pine, a favorite food of Old Griz. Be especially alert late in the year when the bears are fattening up here on whitebark pine nuts for their winter sleep.

Owl Creek is the mirror image of Moose Creek. Instead of climbing steeply through a canyon and then mellowing out for a gentle push to the top, Owl Creek drops sharply at the top and then goes into a gentle open valley. Owl Creek is a gigantic meadow with lots of great campsites and probably more moose than Moose Creek and more berries than Berry Creek. You have two stream crossings (one on Owl Creek and one on Berry Creek)—again, sorry, no footbridges.

When you reach the junction with the cutoff trail to Berry Creek, go right (east) and ford Berry Creek before it merges with Owl Creek. From this point, Berry Creek goes into a narrow canyon. The trail climbs way above the waterway and stays there for about 4 miles until it drops down to the junction with the Webb Canyon Trail. Now, retrace your steps back to the Glade Creek Trailhead.

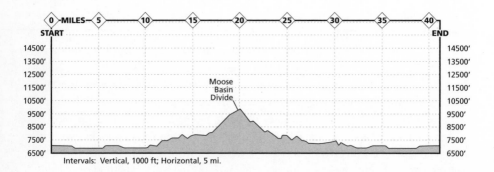

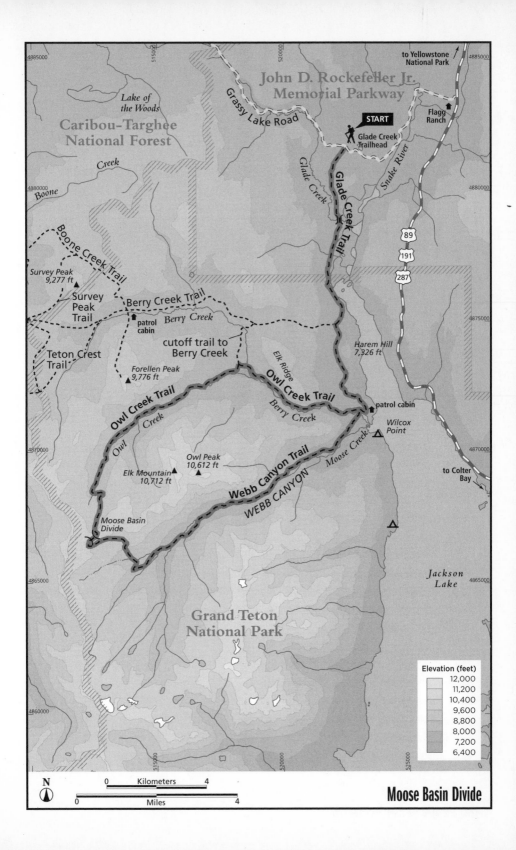

Taking in the vistas on Moose Basin Divide.

Key Points

1.5   Cross the Glade Creek footbridge.

2.0   Break out into a big meadow.

3.5   Park boundary.

4.9   Junction with Berry Creek Trail; turn left.

8.0   Jackson Lake, patrol cabin, and Owl Creek Trail junction; turn right.

8.1   Junction with Webb Canyon Trail; turn left and ford creek.

9.1   Webb Canyon.

19.1   Moose Basin Divide and Owl Creek Trail.

29.1   Cutoff trail to Berry Creek; turn right.

33.1   Junction with Webb Canyon Trail; turn left.

33.2   Jackson Lake and patrol cabin.

36.3   Junction with Berry Creek Trail; turn right.

37.7   Park boundary.

41.2   Glade Creek Trailhead.

Suggested itinerary:

First night: Lower Moose Creek before entering Webb Canyon.

Second night: Moose Basin.

Third night: About halfway down Owl Creek.

Fourth night: Jackson Lake shoreline north of patrol cabin.

Options: You can cut 16 miles off your trip by getting a boat ride or taking a canoe across Jackson Lake from Leeks Marina to Wilcox Point. Be sure to go early in the morning and in good weather. You do not want to get caught in a storm on Jackson Lake. You can also take the loop in reverse, but I believe the hill is more precipitous on the Owl Creek side, and it's 14 miles uphill instead of 11 from the Owl Creek/Webb Canyon Trails junction.

Hiking through the monstrous meadow lining Owl Creek.

You can also go back via the Berry Creek cutoff trail instead of taking the last 4 miles down Berry Creek to the patrol cabin. This only adds about a mile to your trip, but it does mean a big climb to get over a ridge.

Side trip: There are several appealing off-trail side trips in the alpine country on both sides of Moose Basin Divide.

Camping: This is an open camping area, so you may set up a no-trace camp anywhere along this route, before or after entering the park, but you need a permit after crossing the park boundary. It won't be difficult to find scenic campsites, especially at Owl Creek and upper Moose Creek. You can find a good camp in the low country around the patrol cabin or by going up the Webb Canyon Trail for less than a mile. Once in Webb Canyon, however, campsites are marginal. When you break out of the canyon, campsites are plentiful and very scenic. Likewise, when you drop down into Owl Creek, it's easy to find a five-star campsite, but campsites are scarce in the section between the cutoff trail to Berry Creek and the patrol cabin.

Grand Teton Trail Finder

	EASY	MODERATE	HARD
Backcountry Lanes	1 Phelps Lake 6 Leigh Lake 7 Bradley Lake 9 String Lake 10 Taggart Lake 23 Swan Lake and Heron Pond	2 Marion Lake 12 Bearpaw and Trapper Lakes 13 Surprise and Amphitheater Lakes 14 Jenny Lake 15 Holly Lake 18 Valley Trail 27 Hermitage Point 29 Two Ocean Lake 31 Emma Matilda Lake	5 The Teton Crest 17 Lake Solitude 19 Paintbrush Divide
Along Streams	32 Glade Creek	3 Rendezvous Mountain and Granite Canyon 11 Garnet Canyon 16 Cascade Canyon	4 Death Canyon and the Mount Hunt Divide 19 Paintbrush Divide 34 Jackass Pass 35 Moose Basin Divide
Through Alpine Country		3 Rendezvous Mountain and Granite Canyon 13 Surprise and Amphitheater Lakes	4 Death Canyon and the Mount Hunt Divide 5 The Teton Crest 19 Paintbrush Divide 20 The Grand Teton Loop 34 Jackass Pass 35 Moose Basin Divide
Really Flat Trails	9 String Lake 21 Lakeshore Trail 23 Swan Lake and Heron Pond	12 Bearpaw and Trapper Lakes 14 Jenny Lake 26 Willow Flats Loop 18 Valley Trail 27 Hermitage Point 32 Glade Creek	

	EASY	MODERATE	HARD
Overnight Backpacking Trips	**1** Phelps Place **6** Leigh Lake **32** Glade Creek **7** Bradley Lake **9** String Lake **10** Taggart Lake **23** Swan Lake and Heron Pond	**2** Marion Lake **12** Bearpaw and Trapper Lakes **15** Holly Lake **18** Valley Trail **27** Hermitage Point **33** Elk Ridge	**3** Rendezvous Mountain and Granite Canyon **4** Death Canyon and the Mount Hunt Divide **5** The Teton Crest **17** Lake Solitude **19** Paintbrush Divide **20** The Grand Teton Loop **34** Jackass Pass **35** Moose Basin Divide
Early Season Hikes	**1** Phelps Lake **6** Leigh Lake **7** Bradley Lake **9** String Lake **10** Taggart Lake **21** Lakeshore Trail **22** Christian Pond **23** Swan Lake and Heron Pond **24** Willow Flats Shuttle **26** Willow Flats Loop	**12** Bearpaw and Trapper Lakes **14** Jenny Lake **18** Valley Trail **27** Hermitage Point **29** Two Ocean Lake **32** Glade Creek	**31** Emma Matilda Lake

Author's Favorite Hikes

For Photography
- **4** Death Canyon and the Mount Hunt Divide
- **5** The Teton Crest
- **6** Leigh Lake
- **19** Paintbrush Divide
- **20** The Grand Teton Loop
- **27** Hermitage Point

For High-Altitude Scenery
- **5** The Teton Crest
- **13** Surprise and Amphitheater Lakes
- **19** Paintbrush Divide
- **20** The Grand Teton Loop
- **35** Moose Basin Divide

For Wildlife Viewing
- **8** Moose Ponds
- **22** Christian Ponds
- **25** Swan Lake and Heron Pond

For Wildflowers
- **3** Rendezvous Mountain and Granite Canyon
- **15** Holly Lake
- **19** Paintbrush Divide
- **35** Moose Basin Divide

For Hikers Who Want a Really Flat Trail
- **6** Leigh Lake
- **25** Swan Lake and Heron Pond
- **27** Hermitage Point

For Hikers Who Want a Really Easy Day Hike
- **6** Leigh Lake
- **9** String Lake
- **21** Lakeshore Trail
- **23** Swan Lake and Heron Pond

For Hikers Who Want a Moderate Day Hike
- **12** Bearpaw and Trapper Lakes
- **27** Hermitage Point

Preserving Grand Teton

The Grand Teton Natural History Association

This association is a nonprofit organization founded to assist with educational, historical, and scientific programs in and around Grand Teton National Park. The association operates bookstores in the park and in the nearby National Elk Refuge and Bridger-Teton National Forest. When you buy a book, video, or map from one of these bookstores, the profits go to benefit educational and interpretive programs in the park. Your purchase also supports the publication of educational brochures available at information counters and entrance stations.

You can obtain a mail-order catalog of products offered by the association by writing to Grand Teton Natural History Association, P.O. Box 170, Moose, WY 83012. You can also visit www.grandtetonpark.org for more information.

Afterword: The Value of Guidebooks

It has been whispered here and there—usually by "locals"—that books like this are a bad idea. The theory goes something like this: Guidebooks bring more people into the wilderness; more people cause more environmental damage, and the wildness we all seek gradually evaporates.

I used to think like that, too. And here's why I changed my mind.

When I wrote and published my first guidebook in 1979 (*Hiking Montana*), some of my hiking buddies disapproved. Since then, I've published nearly a hundred hiking guides, and I'm very proud of it. I also hope these books have greatly increased wilderness use.

Experienced hikers tend to have a lofty attitude toward the inexperienced masses. They think anybody who wants to backpack can buy a topo map and compass and find their own way through the wilderness. But the fact is most beginning hikers want a guide. Sometimes new hikers prefer a real, live guide to show them the way and help them build confidence, but most of the time they can get by with a trail guide like this one.

All Falcon hiking guides (and most guidebooks published by other publishers) encourage wilderness users to respect and support the protection of wild country. Sometimes, this is direct editorializing. Sometimes, this invitation takes the more subtle form of simply helping people experience wilderness. And it's a rare person who leaves the wilderness without a firmly planted passion for wild country—and a desire to vote for more of it.

In classes on backpacking taught for the Yellowstone Institute, I have taken hundreds of people into the wilderness. Many of them had on a backpack for the first time. Many of them were not at first convinced that we need more wilderness, but they were all convinced when they arrived back at the trailhead. Many, many times, I've seen it happen without saying a single word about wilderness.

It doesn't take preaching. Instead, we just need to get people out into the wilderness where the essence of wildness sneaks up on them and takes root—before you know it, the ranks of those who support wilderness has grown.

But what about overcrowding? Yes, it's a problem in many places and probably is in parts of Grand Teton National Park. The answer to overcrowded, overused wilderness is not limiting use of wilderness and restrictive regulations. The answer is more wilderness. A trampled campsite can be rested and reclaimed, but once roads are built and cabins go up, the land no longer qualifies for wilderness designation.

How can we convince people to support more wilderness when they have never experienced wilderness? In my opinion, we can't. Without the support of people who experience wilderness, there will be no more wilderness.

That's why we need guidebooks. And that's why I changed my mind. I believe guidebooks have done as much to build support for wilderness as pro-wilderness organizations have ever done through political and public relations efforts.

And if that's not enough, here's another reason. All FalconGuides (and again, most guidebooks from other publishers) contain sections on leave-no-trace ethics and wilderness safety. Guidebooks provide an ideal medium for communicating such vital information.

In thirty-five years of backpacking, I have seen dramatic changes in how back-packers care for wilderness. I've seen it go from appalling to exceptional. Today, almost everybody walks softly in the wilderness. And I believe the information contained in guidebooks has been partly responsible for this change.

Having said all that, I hope many thousands of people use this book to enjoy a fun-filled vacation hiking in Grand Teton National Park—and then, of course, vote for wilderness preservation the rest of their lives.

About the Author

Bill Schneider has spent thirty-five years hiking trails all across America. During college in the mid-1960s, he worked on a trail crew in Glacier National Park and became a hiking addict. He spent the 1970s publishing the *Montana Outdoors* magazine for the Montana Department of Fish, Wildlife & Parks while covering as many miles of trails as possible on weekends and holidays. In 1979 Bill and his partner, Mike Sample, founded Falcon Publishing. Since then, he has written twenty books and many magazine articles on wildlife, outdoor recreation, and environmental issues. Bill has also taught classes on bicycling, backpacking, zero-impact camping, and hiking in bear country for the Yellowstone Institute, a nonprofit educational organization in Yellowstone National Park.

In 2000 Bill retired from his position as president of Falcon Publishing (now part of The Globe Pequot Press) after it had grown into the premier publisher of outdoor recreation guidebooks with more than 700 titles in print. He now lives in Helena, Montana, with his wife, Marnie, and works as a publishing consultant and freelance writer.

The author on Moose Basin Divide. ▶